Blouses • Dresses • Skirts • Jackets

The Busy Woman's Fitting Book

by Nancy Zieman with Robbie Fanning

Nancy's Notions, Beaver Dam, WI
Open Chain Publishing, Menlo Park, CA

Co-published in Menlo Park, CA, by Open Chain Publishing
and in Beaver Dam, WI, by Nancy's Notions
ISBN 0-932086-09-8 hardbound
ISBN 0-932086-10-1 softbound
Library of Congress Catalog Card Number 88-063280

Designed by Martha Vercoutere

Illustrations by Pamela S. Poole

Computer aid by Tony Fanning

Cover photo by Skip Ellinger

Proofreading by Judi Maddigan

DEDICATION

To sewing teachers everywhere, amateur and professional, with
gratitude for taking the time to pass on the joy of sewing.
NLZ and RLF

ACKNOWLEDGMENTS

Special thanks to Sarah Bunje of Foster City, CA, and Kathleen Rake
of San Raphael, CA, for reading the manuscript and making invalu-
able suggestions for improvement.

Table of Contents

A LETTER FROM NANCY

Dear Sewing Friend,

Let's face it, most of us dislike fitting. But without the correct fit, our sewing projects just hang in the closet, unworn. As a co-worker puts it, "No fit, no wear!" Fitting is as integral to sewing as winding bobbins.

At the same time, we are all busy. Whether we are students; work fulltime; have children at home, kids at college, an empty nest; or are responsible for parental care, we all struggle to find time for our work and home responsibilities, as well as for volunteer work and hobbies.

The busier we are, the more simplified we need to make some of our routine tasks. For example, we eat simply, freeze meals, and reheat in microwave ovens. Likewise, as sewers, we need to simplify the routine task of fitting patterns.

To make fitting as painless for you as possible, I've followed the KISS principle — Keep It Sweet & Simple — in organizing this book.

You do not need to read the entire book to learn the one alteration you need. Instead, each area on your pattern that needs alteration is explained in its own chapter — bustline, waistline, hipline, sleeve, shoulder and back, length.

Then each alteration chapter is broken into a series of **Fitting Challenges** and **Solutions**.

If you need to fit the bustline, turn to Chapter 3 on Bustline Solutions; identify which alteration you need to make (add, subtract, etc.), match it with the corresponding Fitting Challenge, and learn the Solution, with the alteration steps immediately given.

If you have more than one fitting challenge, Chapter 9 tells how to combine the techniques. Once you understand the concept of this book, explained in the first two chapters, you can use it as you would a cookbook, not a novel, to solve any fitting challenge: turn to the fitting recipe you need, follow the step-by-step directions, and you'll turn out a garment that fits.

Don't spend your valuable sewing time on unneeded hours of fitting. Keep it simple! Robbie and I look forward to showing you how.

Nancy Zieman

The illustrations show how to make these alterations on blouses, dresses, skirts, and jackets. Altering pants needs an extensive step-by-step approach, too long for this book, so I've written how to alter them in a separate book. See last page.

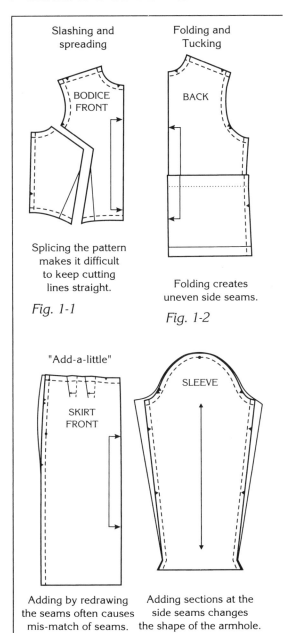

Slashing and spreading

BODICE FRONT

Splicing the pattern
makes it difficult
to keep cutting
lines straight.

Fig. 1-1

Folding and Tucking

BACK

Folding creates
uneven side seams.

Fig. 1-2

"Add-a-little"

SKIRT FRONT

SLEEVE

Adding by redrawing   Adding sections at the
the seams often causes   side seams changes
mis-match of seams.   the shape of the armhole.

Fig. 1-3

Since there are many methods of altering a pattern, you may have learned one particular method or you may be using a combination of ideas. If you are slashing here, folding there, or just plain adding a little everywhere and are not sure which is the best method, let's take a closer look at the pro's and con's of the four main techniques.

1. **Slashing and Spreading** is the most common method of altering patterns (Fig. 1-1). This technique gives additional length and/or width after the pattern has been slashed into sections and spread apart. It is a workable method *if followed accurately*. But many of us are reluctant to slash our patterns, since the grainline is cut and separated, making it difficult to keep the pattern's grain, seam, and cutting lines straight. Another problem occurs with multiple alterations. Splicing the pattern into many different sections for the various alterations can be confusing.

Basically, **Slashing and Spreading** works, but it is time-consuming and the pattern is cut into sections, increasing the chance of error.

2. **Folding and Tucking** a pattern is often used in combination with slashing and spreading (Fig. 1-2). These procedures shorten the pattern length or decrease the width. Again, the seam and pattern lines are easily destroyed and the shape changed. This technique often creates uneven pattern edges.

3. **Add-a-little, Take-off-a-little** is probably the most commonly used method of altering (Fig. 1-3). Changes are made by adding or subtracting at the side seams by simply redrawing the cutting lines. It is extremely easy to add or take away uneven amounts from the pattern, causing the seams to mismatch and the grainline to tip off-grain.

4. **Pivot and Slide Techniques** are the kind used in this book. With this method, the pattern is changed equally on both sides of the grainline. The seam line and design lines will be kept in proportion with the pattern. And all the alterations will be made on a work sheet (wax paper, tissue paper, or a non-woven fabric like Pellon's®Tru-Grid®), keeping the original pattern intact.

Pivot and Slide Alterations are not new to the pattern industry. Pivoting is used by pattern designers to make fashion changes and sliding is used by pattern graders to change pattern sizes.

In this book, **Pivoting** techniques (Fig. 1-4) will be used to increase or decrease the pattern *width* and **Sliding** techniques (Fig. 1-5) will generally be used to add or subtract *length*.

Other than the worksheet material, the only other tools needed are pins, red and black fine-point permanent marking pens, a ruler, a tracing wheel, tape, and a tape measure.

I know you'll enjoy this simple yet accurate approach to fitting. **Pivot and Slide Techniques** can solve all your fitting challenges.

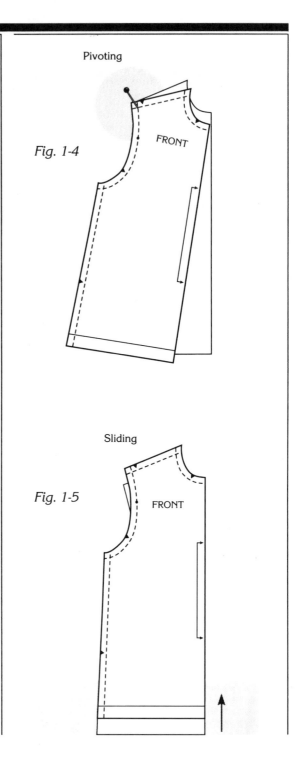

Pivoting

Fig. 1-4

FRONT

Sliding

Fig. 1-5

FRONT

CHAPTER 2
PREPARE TO FIT

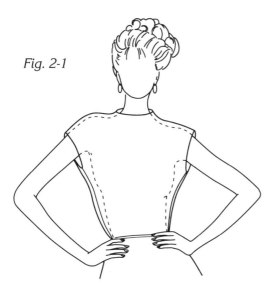

N *In my Nancy's Notions Sewing Catalog, I have added personalized notes, called "Notes From Nancy," next to products that I have found of special interest. In this book, I have also added these notes, giving you added insight that may help you make easier alterations. When you see this symbol along with text like this, it's a Note From Nancy.*

Fig. 2-1

Armhole, shoulder, and neckline are too large if pattern is purchased to fit a fuller bustline.

The Busy Woman's Game Plan

- *Step 1. Pinpoint your correct pattern size and type, according to your Front Width Measurement and body proportions.*
- *Step 2. Buy classic-style patterns and assemble fitting tools.*
- *Step 3. Take your measurements and compare to those on the back of your pattern envelope.*
- *Step 4. Note which areas of the pattern you need to alter— bustline, waistline, hipline, sleeve, shoulder and back, length. Turn to the chapter for that area and find the appropriate Fitting Challenge. (For multiple changes, see Chapter 9.)*
- *Step 5. Use Pivot and Slide Techniques to make changes.*
- *Step 6. Fine-tune the fit.*
- *Step 7. Apply the same alterations to any style of pattern from the same company.*

Pinpoint Your Pattern Size and Type

Traditionally, you have been told to buy blouse, jacket, or top patterns according to your bustline measurement. Yet if your bustline is large in proportion to the rest of your body, a garment made to fit the bustline will gap around the neckline, shoulders, and armholes. (Fig. 2-1)

An easy way to visualize this is to imagine yourself becoming a weight lifter. You would add inches to your back muscles, giving you a bigger bustline measurement. Should you then buy a larger size pattern? No, because your neck and arm areas would not have changed. You merely need to enlarge your usual pattern size at the bustline.

One of the easiest areas on a pattern to alter is the bustline; the more difficult areas to alter and fit are the shoulders, neckline, and armholes. Therefore, rather than buying a pattern to fit the bustline, it is more logical to buy a pattern *to fit the shoulder area.*

This method of buying a pattern is also more practical. If weight is gained or lost, the shoulder, neck, and armhole areas generally do not change. The same pattern size can be altered to fit a relatively larger or smaller you.

Front Width Measurement

To pinpoint your pattern size, take the **Front Width Measurement**. Most of us are familiar with the Back Width Measurement, taken across the back to see if the garment will be too tight or too large. The **Front Width Measurement**, taken across the front of the figure, is the complement of the Back Width Measurement. (Fig. 2-2)

To take this measurement, find the crease in your skin where your arm meets your body. Measure *above* the end of the crease across the front to the end of the other crease. Round off the measurement to the nearest half inch. It is best to have someone help you take this measurement, assuring accuracy.

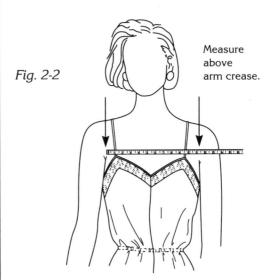

The Front Width Measurement may seem awkward to measure. Be sure to have someone help you take this measurement while you are wearing only a slip (so she can see your arm creases).

Fig. 2-2

Measure above arm crease.

Front width measurement

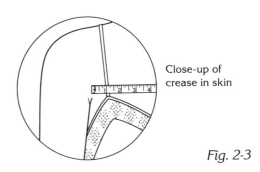

Close-up of crease in skin

Fig. 2-3

FRONT WIDTH FITTING CHART

Front width	12	12½	13	13½	14	14½	15	15½	16	16½	17	17½
Misses' size	6	8	10	12	14	16	18	20	22			
Junior size	5	7	9	11	13	15						
Half-size size			10½	12½	14½	16½	18½	20½	22½	24½		
Women's size							38	40	42	44	46	48

Unfortunately, the Front Width Measurement and the corresponding sizing are not written on the back of the pattern envelope. But the sizing is easy to remember. The sizes change every half inch. The chart above clarifies the sizing.

N N *If you are having a difficult time taking the Front Width Measurement and can't decide which of two measurements to use, go with the smaller measurement. Remember, it is easier to fit the bustline—to make it larger—but more difficult to fit the upper body.*

You may be pleasantly surprised by the results of the Front Width Measurement. It is very common that someone who has been sewing, say, a size 20 to fit her bust, will find out that she is actually a size 12.

Keep your Front Width Measurement and your new pattern size written on a card in your purse, so you can buy the right size patterns in the future.

If you're at the fabric store without such a card and you can only remember your Front Width Measurement, but not what size pattern it translates to, here's the key:

A Front Width Measurement of 14" equals a Misses' size 14.

For every half inch larger or smaller, buy one size larger or smaller pattern.

For example, if you measure 13-1/2", buy a Misses' size 12. If you measure 14-1/2", buy a Misses' size 16.

Now that you know your Front Width Measurement, you have a choice of which type of pattern to buy—Misses', Women's, etc. For example, if your Front Width Measurement is 13-1/2", you could buy a Misses' 12, a Junior 11, or a Half-size 12-1/2. Here's how these pattern types differ.

Misses' Size:

The Front Width Measurement is calculated for this size range. Misses' is a well-proportioned and -developed figure about 5'5" to 5'6" tall, with a B cup size.

Junior Size:

If you normally wear Junior sizes and measure for a Misses' size 8, purchase the corresponding Junior size 7. Junior patterns are designed for well-proportioned, shorter-waisted figures about 5'4" to 5'5", with an A-B cup size.

Half-Size:

If you usually purchase Half-size patterns and are comfortable with the proportions, keep on doing so. Half-size patterns have more room allotted in the bust, waist, and hip, with shorter length proportions, made for figures between 5'2" to 5'4", with a C cup size.

To determine your Half-size pattern, again use your Front Width Measurement. If it is, for example, 14-1/2", you would buy a Misses' size 16 or a Half-size 16-1/2.

Women's:

The Women's figure type is the same height as the Misses' (5'5"-5'6"), but is fuller and larger at the bust (D cup), waist, and hips. Again, use the Front Width Measurement and translate this measurement to a Women's size. If your measurement corresponds to a Misses' size 22 (Front Width Measurement of 16") but your figure type fits the Women's category, purchase the Women's size 42.

 Do not worry if your bust, waist, hip, or back waist length are not the same as those in the charts. This book will teach you how to easily alter the pattern.

Choose a Classic-style Pattern

For your first fitting project with **Pivot and Slide Techniques**, choose a classic-style blouse, skirt, dress, or jacket. By classic, I mean:

- set-in sleeves with no dropped shoulders
- shoulder seams, with no yoke over the shoulders (a decorative front or back yoke is fine)
- no excessive gathering, tucking, or pleating on the sleeves or body
- comfortably fit jacket, not over-sized
- a straight, A-line, or bias-cut skirt without excessive fullness

At first, avoid patterns with numerous pattern pieces and great sewing detail. These alterations can, of course, be made on all types of patterns, but be easy on yourself for this first attempt at what may be, for you, a new way of altering and fitting. Remember, KISS!

Once you can alter classic styles with **Pivot and Slide Techniques**, you'll have the knowledge and experience to alter any style, including highly detailed or extremely over-sized or form-fitting styles.

Misses'	Inches								
Size	6	8	10	12	14	16	18	20	22
Front width	**12**	**12½**	**13**	**13½**	**14**	**14½**	**15**	**15½**	**16**
Bust	30½	31½	32½	34	36	38	40	42	44
Waist	23	24	25	26½	28	30	32	34	36
Hip	32½	33½	34½	36	38	40	42	44	46
Back Waist Length	15½	15¾	16	16¼	16½	16¾	17	17¼	17½

Junior	Inches					
Size	5	7	9	11	13	15
Front width	**12**	**12½**	**13**	**13½**	**14**	**14½**
Bust	30	31	32	33½	35	37
Waist	22½	23½	24½	25½	27	29
Hip	32	33	34	35½	37	39
Back Waist Length	15	15¼	15½	15¾	16	16¼

Half-size	Inches							
Size	10½	12½	14½	16½	18½	20½	22½	24½
Front width	**13**	**13½**	**14**	**14½**	**15**	**15½**	**16**	**16½**
Bust	33	35	37	39	41	43	45	47
Waist	27	29	31	33	35	37½	40	42½
Hip	35	37	39	41	43	45½	48	50½
Back Waist Length	15	15¼	15½	15¾	15⅞	16	16⅛	16¼

Women's	Inches					
Size	38	40	42	44	46	48
Front width	**15**	**15½**	**16**	**16½**	**17**	**17½**
Bust	42	44	46	48	50	52
Waist	35	37	39	41½	44	46½
Hip	44	46	48	50	52	54
Back Waist Length	17¼	17⅜	17½	17⅝	17¾	17⅞

Classic pattern styles are available in every pattern book; look for "Fashion Basic" and "Busy Woman's Sewing Patterns™" from McCall's, "Basic Very Easy Vogue," "Jiffy" from Simplicity, "In-Ann-Instant" from Stretch & Sew, and "Burda Super-Easy."

N **N** *At first, it is easier to fit a pattern with a minimum of pattern pieces, but please don't buy a fitting-shell pattern. In my mind, making a fitting shell is a waste of time, since this garment will never be worn. The quality of the fit can just as easily be checked on a classic-style pattern—plus you've used your precious time to add to your wardrobe.*

Understand Design Ease

The ease in patterns gives us both comfort and fashion; ease amount varies with each pattern, depending upon the style and the type of fabric for which the pattern was designed. (Fig. 2-5) Design ease is the difference between the sizing measurements on the back of the pattern, which apply to all patterns from that company, and the actual measurements of your tissue pattern, which apply only to the style you bought.

You may have learned an alteration method that is a complicated procedure of measuring the pattern tissue, subtracting the measurements on the back of the pattern, adding ease to your measurements, subtracting those—on and on until the subject of fitting patterns makes you want to run in the opposite direction.

Classic jacket   Fig. 2-4

Classic blouse and skirt

Design ease

Fig. 2-5

For the most part, **do not** spend time measuring each pattern tissue to determine its ease. Once you know what alterations you need on a classic-style pattern, **you will automatically make those same changes on every pattern from that company**, no matter what the style. This knowledge is a wonderful time-saver for the busy woman!

Only check the pattern tissue measurements if you think an **over-sized style** may have too many inches of ease or a **form-fitting style** may not have enough ease for your taste in fit. Here's how to check the ease.

Ease Check

For woven fabrics, the minimum ease requirements are:

Bust...................................3" to 4"

Waist.............................1/2" to 1"

Hip...................................2" to 4"

Designers use these amounts as guidelines, but vary the actual ease to produce fashionable patterns. A loose-fitting jacket, for example, might have as much as 6-8" of bust ease.

It's easy to check the design ease allowed in the bust, waist, and hip. Here I've checked the bustline as the example.

1. Pin the pattern pieces together at the underarm, stacking the stitching lines.

2. Hold the tape measure with the 1" end in your left hand. Fold the 1" end of the tape measure until it meets your bust measurement from the back of the pattern envelope. For example, if you are a Misses' size 12, the bust measurement is 34".

3. Place the folded end of the tape measure across the bust area, measuring from the stitching (or fold) line of the center front to the stitching (or fold) line of the center back.

4. The gap between the 1" end of the tape measure and the stitching (or fold) line of the center back is **half of the ease**: double this measurement to find out the total design ease. (Fig. 2-6)

Remember, only check ease for tight- or loose-fitting styles.

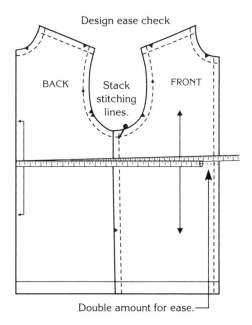 *Both Vogue and McCall patterns print the actual pattern width on the tissue, making the ease extremely easy to determine.*

Design ease check

BACK   Stack stitching lines.   FRONT

Double amount for ease.—

Fig. 2-6

Compare Your Measurements

Now that you've bought your classic-style pattern and assembled your fitting tools, it's time to compare your measurements to the back of the pattern envelope. Each chapter in this book tells you exactly how and where to measure yourself. At this point, just determine whether you need to alter or not. The four areas given on the pattern envelope are bust, waist, hip, and back waist length. Fill in the appropriate measurements in the chart below. You will also need to check 1) sleeve width and 2) pattern length, but these measurements are not given on the pattern envelope.

Find the Appropriate Fitting Challenge

You now know what areas on the pattern need to be altered and what chapters contain that information. Find the Fitting Challenge in each chapter that asks the question you need answered—i.e., "How do I increase the bustline?" Each Solution shows you exactly how to pivot or slide for that alteration.

You do not need to read the whole book to make the alterations you need, but please read through the first Fitting Challenge in Chapter 3. You will then understand how to pivot and slide for your needed alterations.

Congratulations! You're on your way toward perfect fit.

YOUR PERSONAL FITTING CHART

Date:

Front Width Measurement:

Pattern Type:

Pattern Size:

	Bust Chapter 3	**Waist** Chapter 4	**Hip** Chapter 5	**Back Waist** Chapter 8
Pattern Envelope Measurement				
—Your Measurement				
=Difference (+/-)				
Alter? (Yes or No)				

Notes: 1) As you alter for Bust, Waist, and/or Hip, also check: Sleeve (Chapter 6); Shoulder/Back (Chapter 7); and Length (Chapter 8).
2) For larger cup sizes, see Chapter 3.
3) For multiple alterations, see Chapter 9.

CHAPTER 3
BUSTLINE SOLUTIONS

How do I:

- *increase the bustline?*
- *decrease the bustline?*
- *alter the bustline on a blazer with a side panel?*
- *alter the bustline on a pattern with a front or back yoke?*
- *raise or lower a bustline dart?*
- *add a dart?*
- *increase the dart size?*

If you have pinpointed your pattern size using the **Front Width Measurement** to a smaller size than usual, you will have a better fit in the shoulders, armholes, and neckline. Yet you will probably need to increase the bustline, a change you may never have made before. As explained earlier, it is much easier to increase the bustline than to change the fit of the shoulders, neckline, and armhole. In this chapter you'll see how to make the bustline changes on classic and stylized patterns.

Perhaps, instead, your fitting concerns center around decreasing the bustline, repositioning the dart, or even deepening the dart. If any of these areas are your fitting problems, the solutions will be given in this chapter.

Prepare to Fit

1. Cut out the front and back pattern pieces along the *cutting lines*. Press the pattern tissue pieces with a dry iron.

2. Cut two worksheets (lengths of wax paper, tissue paper, or a non-woven fabric like Pellon's® Tru-Grid®) as long as each pattern piece. In most cases, the worksheet does not need to be as wide as the pattern piece.

3. Organize your fitting tools:

- red and black permanent marking pens, fine-point
- pins
- tape measure
- tracing wheel (for wax paper)
- ruler
- tape

N *Remember that all alterations will be made on a worksheet and then the worksheet will be attached to the pattern. Making the changes on another piece of paper keeps the original pattern intact.*

Measure Your Bustline (Fig. 3-2)

To accurately measure the bustline:

- Measure around the fullest part of the bustline, keeping the tape measure parallel to the floor.
- For best results, have someone measure you, placing a thumb or finger underneath the tape measure to prevent the measurement from being taken too tightly.
- Measure to the closest 1/2".

Fig. 3-2

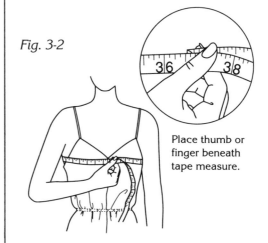

Place thumb or finger beneath tape measure.

Calculate the Change

Whether you need to increase or decrease the bustline, use these simple steps to determine the amount of the alteration.

1. Compare your bustline measurement to the bustline measurement for your size on the pattern back. The difference between the two measurements equals the alteration you must make.

Actual Measurement............. 37"

Pattern Envelope .... 34"

Alteration............................... 3"

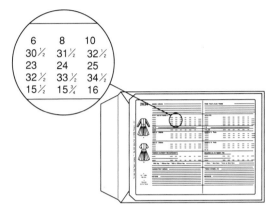

N N *If you need to add more than 4" total (or 1" per side seam) to the bustline width, also read Chapter 6 on Sleeves, page 60, about adding Extra Extensions.*

2. Divide the alteration amount by 4, the total number of cut edges at both side seams. (In the above example, 3/4" would be added to each cut edge.)

To quickly determine the alteration needed at each cut edge, make a fraction. Place the alteration amount, in this case 3, over the number of cut edges, 4. Presto: 3/4" is the amount per edge!

Throughout the book we show the original outline of the pattern with a solid line and the changed outline with a dashed line. To avoid confusion about which line to use when you are making the changes on your worksheet, use a fine-point black pen for the original outline and a fine-point red pen for the changed outline.

N N *If you are using wax paper as a worksheet, you can use a tracing wheel to transfer grainlines and notches to the worksheet. The spokes of the tracing wheel will perforate the wax paper. Experiment to see if you need to put a lightly padded surface (such as flannel or wool yardage) under the wax paper. Sometimes the spoke marks do not show as easily when you trace directly onto a hard surface.*

Bustline Fitting Challenge #1: "How do I increase the bustline?"

Solution:

1. Place the front pattern piece on top of a worksheet. With the black permanent marker, outline the pattern cutting lines on the worksheet.

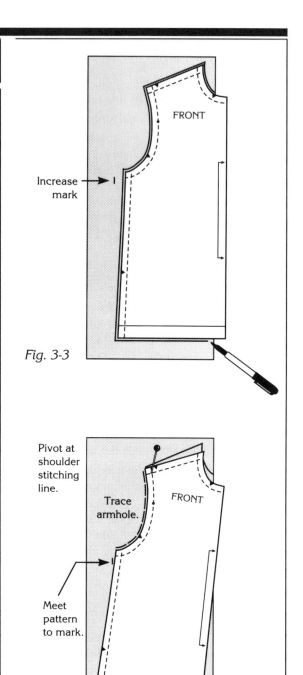

Don't worry if the wax paper isn't wide enough for your pattern. The worksheet doesn't have to reach all the way to the center front. It only needs to extend to the left as much as you need for the alteration.

2. Measure *out* from the cutting line at the underarm area the needed increase. Place a mark on the worksheet. (Fig. 3-3)

3. Anchor the pattern by placing a pin at the shoulder where the stitching lines cross. (This is a pivot point.)

A pivot point is like a fulcrum on a pendulum, the anchor that allows the pendulum to swing. In this case, the pivot point allows the pattern to swing.

4. **Pivot** the pattern so the *cutting line* meets the increase mark.

5. With the red pen, outline the new armhole cutting line of the pivoted pattern on the worksheet. (Fig. 3-4)

6. Keep the pattern pivoted. Move the pivot pin to the underarm where the stitching lines cross.

7. **Pivot** the pattern so the *cutting line* meets the original outlined waistline.

Increase mark

Fig. 3-3

FRONT

Pivot at shoulder stitching line.

Trace armhole.

FRONT

Meet pattern to mark.

Fig. 3-4

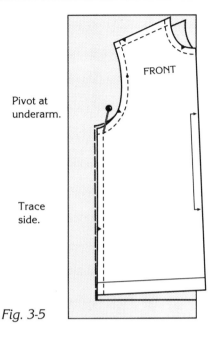

Pivot at underarm.

Trace side.

Fig. 3-5

FRONT

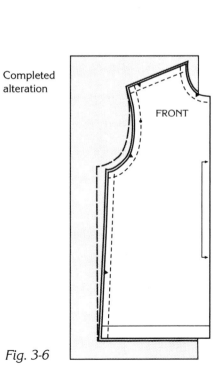

Completed alteration

Fig. 3-6

FRONT

8. Outline the new cutting line between the underarm and the waistline on the worksheet. (Fig. 3-5)

9. Tape the pattern to the worksheet, matching the original outline to the old pattern cutting lines. (Fig 3-6) Cut out the pattern, following the new outline.

10. Apply the same steps to the side seams of the back pattern piece.

When the pattern is placed back in the original position, notice the alteration: the bust width is increased, but the armhole is the same size as the original pattern. Plus, your pattern is still intact.

N_N *Just a reminder: do not pivot at the bustline more than 1" per cut edge. See Chapter 6, page 60, for how to add Extra Extensions.*

N_N *On a grandfather clock, the pendulum swings both ways and so can the swing of a pattern. The pattern swings outside the cutting line to increase the width, or inside the cutting line to decrease the width.*

Bustline Fitting Challenge #2: "How do I decrease the bustline?"

Solution:

1. Place the front pattern piece on top of a worksheet. With the black permanent marker, outline the cutting lines on the worksheet.

2. Measure and mark *in* from the *cutting line* at the underarm the needed decrease.

3. Anchor the pattern by placing a pin at the shoulder where the stitching lines cross. (This is a pivot point.)

4. **Pivot** the pattern so the *cutting line* meets the decrease mark.

5. With the red pen, outline the armhole cutting line of the pivoted pattern on the worksheet. (Fig. 3-7)

6. Keep the pattern pivoted. Move the pivot pin to the underarm where the stitching lines cross.

7. **Pivot** the pattern so the *cutting line* meets the original outlined waistline.

8. Trace the new cutting line between the underarm and the waistline on the worksheet. (Fig. 3-8)

9. Tape the pattern to the worksheet, matching the original outline to the old pattern cutting lines. Cut out the pattern, following the new outline.

10. Apply the same steps to the side seams of the back pattern piece.

Note: When decreasing any area of the pattern, the new cutting line will be inside the original pattern. Either place the worksheet on top of the pattern and trim away the excess pattern tissue, or fold back the original pattern so as not to cut into it.

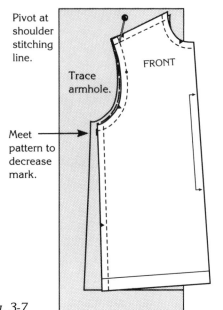

Pivot at shoulder stitching line.

Trace armhole.

FRONT

Meet pattern to decrease mark.

Fig. 3-7

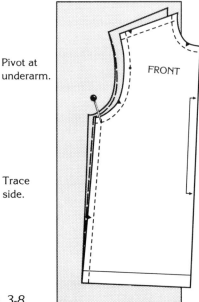

Pivot at underarm.

FRONT

Trace side.

Fig. 3-8

Bustline Fitting Challenge #3: "How do I alter the bustline on a blazer with a side panel?"

Solution:

Remember, we are still only altering four cut edges, even though there is an extra pattern piece. We don't increase the width of the side panel piece.

1. Pin the three jacket pieces (front, side panel, back) together at the underarm seam, stacking stitching lines.

2. Extend a line from the underarm of the side panel to the front and back pieces. (Fig. 3-9) Unpin the pattern pieces. Remove the side panel pattern piece.

3. Place worksheets under the front and back pattern pieces. With the black pen, outline the armholes and side seams of the patterns on the worksheets.

4. Measure *out* from the *cutting line* the needed increase (or *in* for the decrease) across from the underarm line on the front and back. (Fig. 3-10)

5. On both the front and back, place a pin at the shoulder pivot point. **Pivot** the pattern so the *cutting line* meets the bustline increase mark.

6. With the red pen, trace the armhole and under the arm to the underarm line. (Fig. 3-11)

7. Keep the pattern pivoted and move the pivot pin to the stitching line at the underarm line.

8. **Pivot** the pattern inward so the *cutting line* meets the outline at the waistline. Trace the new underarm seam. (Fig. 3-12)

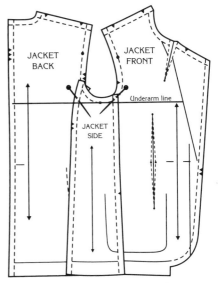

Pin stitching lines together at underarm.
Draw underarm line perpendicular to grain.

Fig. 3-9

Fig. 3-10

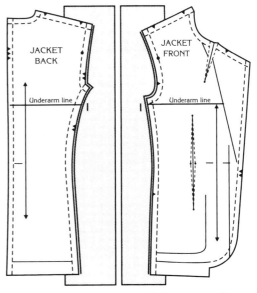

Measure out increase on worksheet across from underarm line. Trace armhole side of pattern.

Pivot pattern
to meet
increase mark.

Trace armhole
and under
the arm to
underarm line.

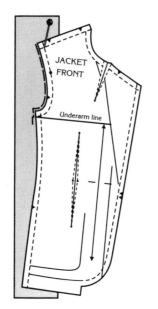

Fig. 3-11

Move pivot
pin to stitching
line at underarm.

Pivot pattern
to meet the
outline at
waistline.

Trace new
underarm
seam.

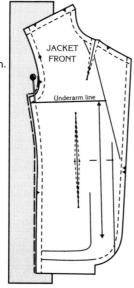

Fig. 3-12

Completed
alteration for
jacket front.

Repeat procedure
for jacket back.

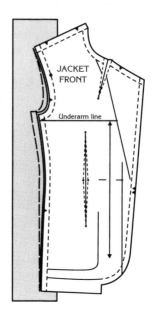

Fig. 3-13

Completed
alteration
for jacket
back

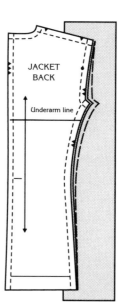

Fig. 3-14

Side Panel

While the altered front and back pattern pieces may appear higher and more binding at the underarm, it's only an illusion. If you match the new armhole cutting lines to the old armhole lines, they will be the same, yet the bustline is wider. How? We've snuck some extra fabric into the side seam length when pivoting. Therefore, we must also lengthen the side panel to match the length of the front and back pieces.

9. On either the back (or front) pattern side seam at the armhole, measure the distance between the original outline and the alteration (Fig. 3-15). Record the amount.

10. With the black pen, outline the side panel on a worksheet. Extend the grainline on the pattern. Draw this extended grainline on the worksheet. From the underarm *cutting line*, measure *up* the amount determined in Step 9.

11. **Slide** the pattern *up* to meet the mark, following the grain line, to meet the mark.

12. With the red pen, trace the raised underarm, across the top, and 1" on each side.

13. Tape the pattern to the worksheet, matching the cutting lines to the original outline. Cut out the pattern, following the new outline (Fig. 3-16).

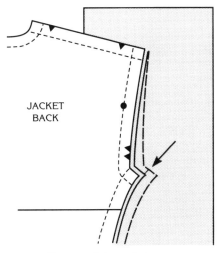

Measure distance between old and new cutting lines.

Fig. 3-15

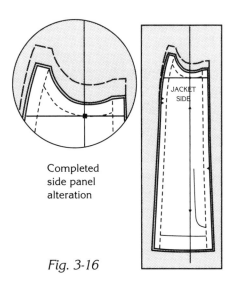

Completed side panel alteration

Fig. 3-16

Bustline Fitting Challenge #4:
"How do I alter the bustline on a pattern with a front or back decorative yoke?"

Solution:

Pivot and Slide Alterations apply to any pattern style. In a decorative yoke style, the bodice is in two pieces. The horizontal seam must be pinned together prior to altering. You'll need four worksheets for this alteration, two for the front and two for the back.

1. Pin the yoke pattern piece to that of the blouse front, stacking stitching lines. (Fig. 3-17)

2. Overlap the two front worksheets 1-1/4", the amount of both seam allowances, and tape together. (Fig. 3-18)

3. Place the pattern pieces on top of the worksheets, matching the stacked seam allowances to the overlapped worksheets. With the black pen, outline the cutting line of the whole pattern on the worksheet. Measure *out* the needed increase from the *cutting line* at the underarm area. (If decreasing, measure *in* from the *cutting line*.)

4. Anchor the pattern by placing a pin where the shoulder and armhole stitching lines cross. (This is a pivot pin.)

5. **Pivot** the pattern so the *cutting line* meets the increase (or decrease) mark.

6. With the red pen, outline the armhole cutting line of the pivoted pattern on the worksheet.

7. Keep the pattern pivoted. Move the pivot pin to the underarm where the stitching lines cross.

Pin pieces together, stacking stitching lines.

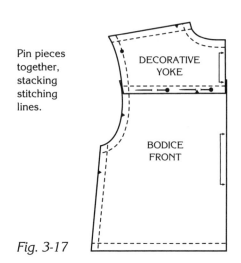

Fig. 3-17

1-1/4" Overlap

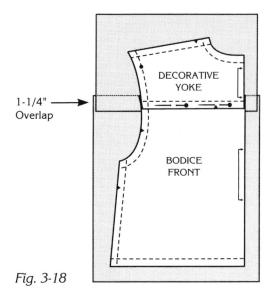

Fig. 3-18

Place patterns on top of worksheet and alter.

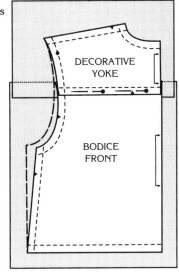

Fig. 3-19

Separate worksheets and patterns.

Attach respective worksheet to pattern.

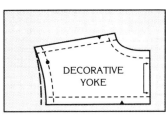

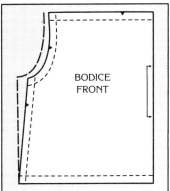

Fig. 3-20

8. **Pivot** the pattern so the *cutting line* meets the original outlined waistline.

9. Outline the cutting line between the underarm and the waistline on the worksheet. (Fig. 3-19)

10. Untape the worksheets; unpin the pattern pieces. Place the respective pattern pieces and worksheets together, matching the original outline to the old pattern cutting lines. Tape the patterns to the worksheets (Fig 3-20).

11. Cut out the pattern, following the new outline.

12. Repeat on the back pattern pieces.

 A common blouse style has a yoke across the shoulder. If you are new to Pivot and Slide Techniques, don't practice on this style. It's more difficult to alter. If you are experienced with Pivot and Slide Techniques, see Chapter 10 for how to alter this style.

Bustline Fitting Challenge #5: "How do I raise or lower a bustline dart?"

This is a simple alteration that involves moving the entire dart up or down, but doesn't otherwise change the length of the pattern.

Calculate the Change

To mark your bustline position on the pattern piece:

1. Pin the shoulder seams of the front and back together, stacking the stitching lines. (See Fig. 3-26.)

2. Put the pattern "on." Pin pattern shoulder seam to your slip strap at the top of the shoulder.

3. Pin the pattern center front to your center front.

4. Slip a scrap of paper under the pattern to protect your slip from the pen bleeding through the pattern. Then use the black pen to mark the fullest part of your bustline on the pattern. Unpin and remove the pattern. Discard the scrap paper. (Fig. 3-21)

Solution:

1. On the pattern front, use a ruler to extend the upper dart leg toward the center front. Measure distance between this extended line and your bustpoint marked on the pattern. Note this measurement on the pattern. (Fig. 3-22)

2. Place a worksheet under the front pattern piece.

3. With the black pen, outline the neckline, shoulder, armhole, and bottom edge of pattern. *Do not* outline the side seam.

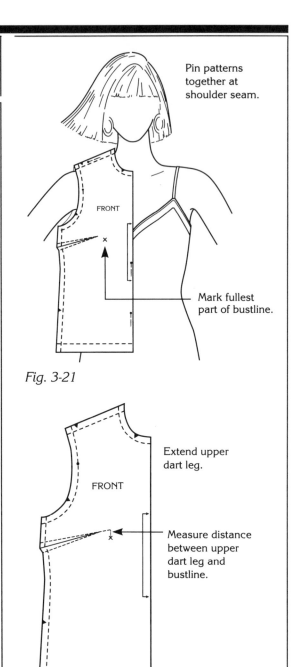

Pin patterns together at shoulder seam.

FRONT

Mark fullest part of bustline.

Fig. 3-21

Extend upper dart leg.

FRONT

Measure distance between upper dart leg and bustline.

Fig. 3-22

Outline neckline, shoulder, armhole, and bottom edge of pattern on worksheet.

Slide pattern down amount measured in Step 1. (Or slide up if raising dart).

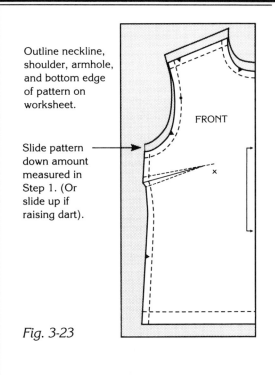

Fig. 3-23

Trace side seam, making hash marks at new dart position.

FRONT

Fig. 3-24

4. If lowering the dart, at the underarm **slide** the pattern *down* the amount noted in Step 1. (**Slide** the pattern *up* if raising the dart.) (Fig. 3-23)

5. Trace the new side seam, making hash marks at side seam to mark the beginning of the dart legs. (Fig. 3-24)

6. Mark the new dart legs on the worksheet, using the dart on the pattern piece as a guide. (The dart is the same; it's just moved up or down, depending on the alteration.)

7. Tape the worksheet on *top* of the pattern so the changed dart is evident.

8. Cut out the pattern, following the new outline. (Fig. 3-25)

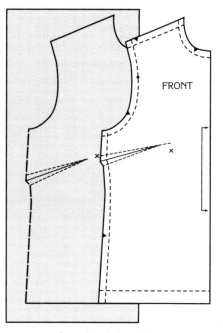

Completed alteration

Fig. 3-25

Bustline Fitting Challenge #6:
"How do I add a dart?"

Solution:

All Misses' patterns are designed to fit a B cup. If you have a larger cup size, you've probably noticed that the waistline usually pulls up and/or bias wrinkles radiate from your underarm to the bustline. On jackets, the center front has a tendency to bow out to the sides. Even though you pivoted to increase for your bust (Bustline Fitting Challenge #1), for larger cup sizes, bustline darts provide additional length and shape. To add a dart to a dartless pattern, use this simple drafting technique.

1. Pin the front and back pattern pieces together at the shoulder seam, stacking the stitching lines. (Fig. 3-26)

2. Tape a worksheet on *top* of the pattern piece below the underarm; extend the worksheet at the side and bottom.

3. Put the pattern "on." Pin the pattern shoulder seam to your slip strap at the top of the shoulder. Pin the pattern center front to your center front.

4. Slip a scrap of paper under the pattern to protect your slip from the pen bleeding through the pattern. Then use the black pen to mark the pattern at the fullest part of the bustline. (Fig. 3-27)

5. At the side seam, fold the pattern to form a bustline dart. (Treat the pattern and worksheet as one.) The fold should be deep enough to allow the center front of the pattern to hang straight and should be whatever angle your body needs. (The angle is unimportant here; we are looking for the proper dart depth for you.) Pin the dart closed.

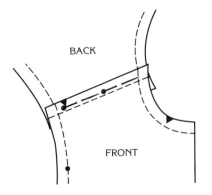

Pin front to back, stacking stitching lines.

Fig. 3-26

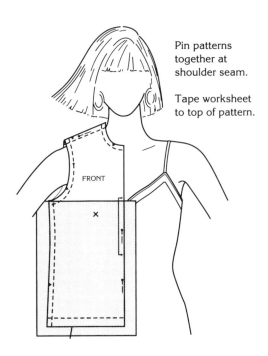

Pin patterns together at shoulder seam.

Tape worksheet to top of pattern.

Pin center front of pattern to your center front. Mark fullest area of figure.

Fig. 3-27

When the pattern is pinned to the center front, it folds or wrinkles at the side seam conforming to the shape of the figure; it doesn't hang perfectly straight as currently illustrated.

6. Unpin and remove the pattern from the figure. Don't unpin the dart until you measure and record the full depth of the dart at the stitching line of the side seam. (The full depth is twice the folded measurement.) (Fig. 3-28)

7. Unpin the dart. Draw Line A on the worksheet from the bust apex (the mark made in Step 4—fullest part of bust) to the side seam, making the line perpendicular to the lengthwise grainline. Line A is merely a starting point. It does not become part of the dart.

8. On the worksheet, draw the first dart leg toward the fullest part of the bustline at an angle beginning 1" below Line A and stopping 1" from the apex of the bustline (Line B).

9. Draw a second dart leg on the worksheet. Measure down from the first dart leg (Line B) the full depth of the dart— the measurement determined in Step 6. Draw a line at an angle from this point to the end of Line B, forming a dart (Line C). (Fig. 3-29)

10. Fold the pattern along the second dart leg (C) to meet the first dart leg (B) to determine the dart underlay.

Note: The side seam ends of the dart legs may not meet with the folded pattern. The next step will fix this.

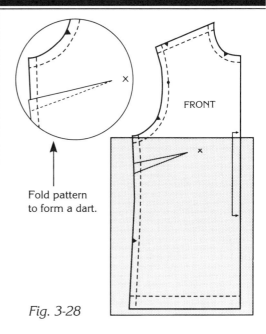

Fold pattern
to form a dart.

FRONT

Fig. 3-28

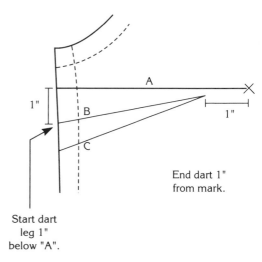

A

1"

B

1"

C

End dart 1"
from mark.

Start dart
leg 1"
below "A".

Fig. 3-29

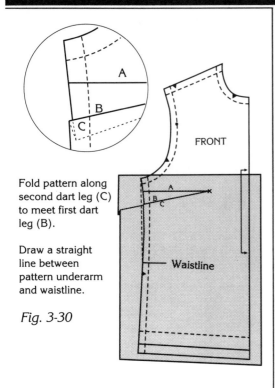

Fold pattern along second dart leg (C) to meet first dart leg (B).

Draw a straight line between pattern underarm and waistline.

Fig. 3-30

FRONT

Waistline

11. With the dart still folded, draw a straight line between the pattern under-arm cutting edge and the waistline cutting edge. Cut the pattern and the worksheet along this line. Unfold. The dart underlay and the length of the dart leg were both made at the same time. (Fig. 3-30)

12. The side seams of the front and back pattern pieces will not match. The side front will be shorter by the amount of the depth of the dart. On the worksheet, add the amount of the depth of the dart to the length across the bottom of the front piece.

13. Tape the pattern to the worksheet, matching the original outline to the old pattern cutting lines. Cut out the pattern, following the new outline. (Fig. 3-31)

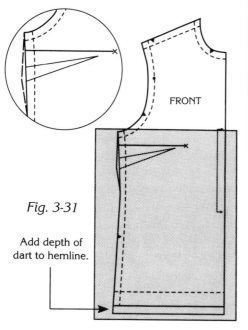

FRONT

Fig. 3-31

Add depth of dart to hemline.

Bustline Fitting Challenge #7: "How do I increase the dart size?"

Solution:

All Misses' patterns are drafted to fit a B cup; Juniors, an A/B cup; Half-sizes, a C cup; and Women's, a D cup. The depth of the dart increases 1/2" per size. You may have the proportions for a Misses' pattern, but need a larger cup size, thus a deeper dart. To deepen an existing dart, add 1/2" per cup size.

1. Place a worksheet under the front pattern. With the black pen, outline the bottom of the pattern and the center front (or center cut edge).

2. **Slide** the pattern *up* the amount needed to deepen the dart. For example, if changing a Misses' size (made to fit a B cup size) to a D cup size, slide the pattern up 1"; if changing to a C cup size, slide the pattern up 1/2".

3. Outline the neckline, shoulder, armhole, and down the side to the first dart leg. Place a hash mark at the dart leg. (Fig. 3-32)

4. **Slide** the pattern *down* to meet the original lower outline of the bottom of the pattern.

5. Place a hash mark at the lower dart leg and continue to outline the side seam. (Fig. 3-33)

6. Tape the pattern to the worksheet, matching the pattern cutting lines to the outline marks *at the shoulder area.*

7. Use the hash mark made in Step 5; draw the new lower dart leg to meet the original dart point. (Fig. 3-34)

8. Treating the worksheet and pattern as one, fold the lower dart leg to meet

Fig. 3-32

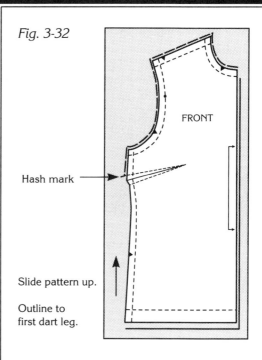

Hash mark →

Slide pattern up.

Outline to first dart leg.

FRONT

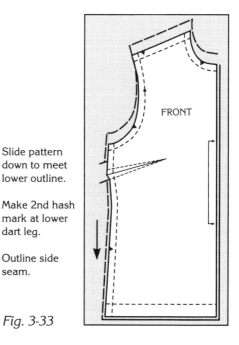

Slide pattern down to meet lower outline.

Make 2nd hash mark at lower dart leg.

Outline side seam.

FRONT

Fig. 3-33

the top leg. Draw a new cutting line between underarm and second dart leg (Fig. 3-35). At the side seam, cut the worksheet following the new cutting line. The dart underlay will be slightly wider due to the deeper dart. (Fig. 3-36)

9. Cut out the pattern, following the new outline.

N **N** ***This alteration deepens the dart while automatically adding the needed length to the center front. You'll be pleased with the ease of making this change and the resulting fit.***

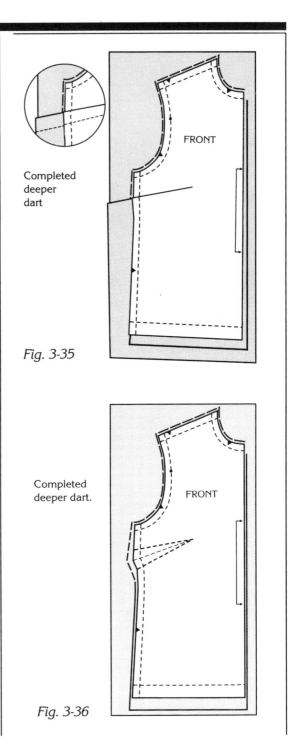

Completed deeper dart

FRONT

Fig. 3-35

Completed deeper dart.

FRONT

Fig. 3-36

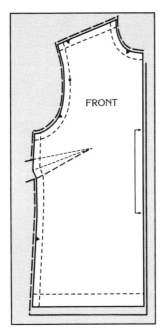

FRONT

Fig. 3-34

CHAPTER 4

WAISTLINE SOLUTIONS

How do I:

- *increase the waistline on a bodice?*
- *decrease the waistline on a bodice?*
- *alter the waistline on a one-piece dress?*
- *alter the waistline on a skirt?*
- *the waistband of a skirt pattern?*

Prepare to Fit

1. Cut out the front and back pattern pieces along the *cutting lines*. Press the pattern tissue pieces with a dry iron.

2. Cut two worksheets (length of wax paper, tissue paper, or a non-woven fabric like Pellon® Tru-Grid®) as long as each pattern piece.

3. Organize fitting tools:
- red and black permanent marking pens, fine-point
- pins
- tape measure
- ruler
- tape
- tracing wheel (optional)

Measure Your Waistline

To accurately measure the waistline:

- Bend to the side. The deepest wrinkle in your skin is the waistline. (Fig. 4-1)
- Measure around your waistline, keeping the tape measure parallel to the floor.
- Place thumb or finger underneath the tape measure to prevent the measurement from being taken too tightly.
- Measure to the closest 1/2". (Fig. 4-2)

Calculate the Change

For a loose garment that isn't fitted at the waistline, such as a shirt or one-piece dress, do not be concerned about altering the waistline of the pattern if you will be increasing the hipline. The hipline increases will usually take care of the waistline. The following width changes should only be made if the waistline is fitted.

1. Compare your waistline measurement to the waistline measurement for your size printed on the pattern back. The difference between the two measurements equals the needed alteration.

Actual Measurement .... 27"

Pattern Envelope .... 25"

Alteration .... 2"

2. Divide the alteration amount by 4, the total number of cut edges at both side seams. (In the example, 2/4" (1/2") would be added to each cut edge.)

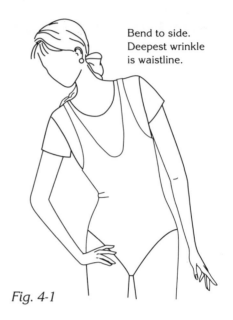

Bend to side. Deepest wrinkle is waistline.

Fig. 4-1

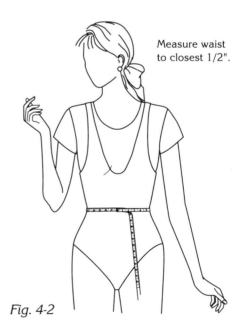

Measure waist to closest 1/2".

Fig. 4-2

Waistline Fitting Challenge #1: "How do I increase the waistline on a bodice?"

Solution:

1. Place the front pattern piece on top of a worksheet. With the black pen, outline the pattern cutting lines.

2. Measure *out* from the waistline *cutting line* the needed increase and mark on the worksheet. (Fig. 4-3)

3. Place a pin at the underarm where the stitching lines cross. **Pivot** the pattern so the *cutting line* meets the increase mark. (Fig. 4-4) With the red pen, outline the new side seam cutting line.

4. Tape the pattern to the worksheet, matching the original outline to the old pattern cutting lines. Cut out the pattern, following the new outline. (Fig. 4-5)

5. Apply same steps to the back piece.

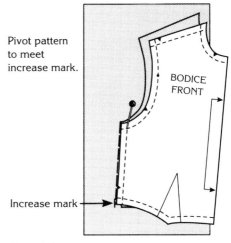

Pivot pattern to meet increase mark.

BODICE FRONT

Increase mark →

Fig. 4-4

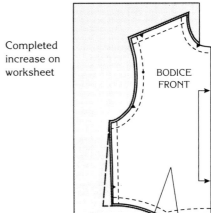

Completed increase on worksheet

BODICE FRONT

Fig. 4-5

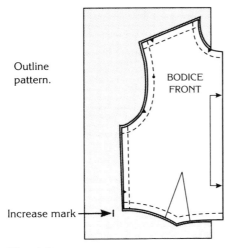

Outline pattern.

BODICE FRONT

Increase mark →

Fig. 4-3

**Waistline Fitting Challenge #2:
"How do I decrease the waistline on a
bodice?"**

Solution:

1. Place the front pattern on top of a worksheet. With a permanent marker, outline the pattern cutting lines.

2. Measure *in* from the waistline cutting line the needed decrease and mark on the worksheet.

3. Place a pin at the underarm where the stitching lines cross. **Pivot** the pattern to meet the decrease mark. (Fig. 4-6)

4. Outline the new side seam cutting line.

5. Tape the pattern to the worksheet, matching the original outline to the old pattern cutting lines. Cut out the pattern, following the new outline. (Fig. 4-7)

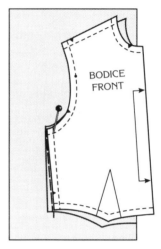

Pivot pattern
to meet
decrease mark.

BODICE
FRONT

Fig. 4-6

N N *When decreasing any area of the pattern, obviously the new cutting line is inside the original pattern. Either place the worksheet on top of the pattern and trim away the excess pattern tissue, or fold back the original pattern so as not to cut into it.*

6. Apply the same steps to the back piece.

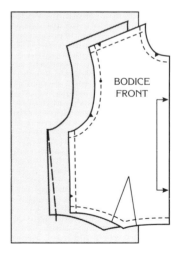

Cut away
the excess
width at the
waistline.

BODICE
FRONT

Fig. 4-7

Waistline Fitting Challenge #3: "How do I alter the waistline on a one-piece dress?"

Solution:

KISS—keep it simple! Don't worry about pivoting. To increase the waistline, merely draw a line from the underarm to the hipline. (The hipline is 9" below the waistline.) (Fig. 4-8)

If your waistline is smaller than the pattern measurement, do not be concerned with this alteration, since the waist is not fitted.

N *Don't overfit your patterns! In other words, do not be concerned with every 1/8" difference and every tiny wrinkle. Overfitting can be exasperating and can make sewing an unhappy experience.*

Waistline Fitting Challenge #4: "How do I alter the waistline on a skirt?"

Solution:

On a skirt or two-piece dress, a combination of **Pivot and Slide Techniques** is used. This alteration is logical, as well as easy.

1. With the black pen, outline the waist, side seam, and bottom cutting lines on a worksheet. (Fig. 4-9) Draw a hipline on your pattern 9" below the waist and perpendicular to the lengthwise grain.

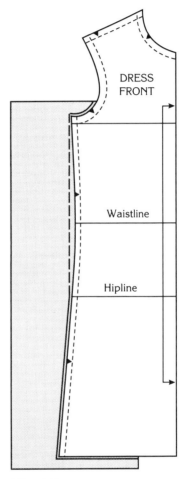

DRESS FRONT

Waistline

Hipline

Fig. 4-8

2. Measure *out* for an increase (or *in* for a decrease). Place a mark on the worksheet at the waistline.

3. **Slide** the pattern horizontally to the waistline mark. (Fig. 4- 9) With the red pen, outline the wider waistline if increasing the waist (or place a hash mark at the narrower waistline mark if decreasing).

4. Place a pin where the waistline and side seam stitching lines cross. **Pivot** the pattern so the *cutting line* meets the original outline at the hipline. Outline the new cutting line between waist and hip. (Fig. 4-9)

5. Tape the pattern to the worksheet, matching the original outline and the old pattern cutting lines. Cut out the pattern, following the new outline.

6. Apply the same techniques to the back piece.

Completed
increase
on worksheet

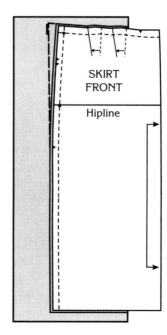

Fig. 4-10

Slide pattern
to increase
mark.

Pivot pattern
to meet
outline at
hipline.

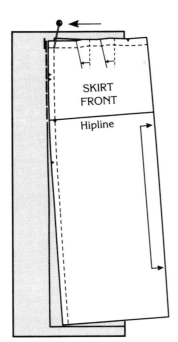

Fig. 4-9

Completed
decrease
on worksheet

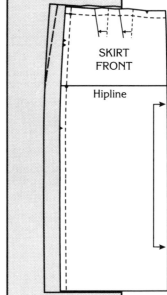

Fig. 4-11

Waistline Fitting Challenge #5: "How do I alter the waistband of a skirt pattern?"

If you need to increase or decrease the waistline of the skirt itself, you must also change the waistband pattern piece. We do this by **sliding** the pattern. Although it may seem easier to add or subtract a section to the end of the waistband, rather than sliding the pattern, this procedure doesn't allow the notches of the waistband to align to the notches in the skirt pattern.

Calculate the Change

1. Make the same increase or decrease on the waistband piece as was made on the skirt waistline.

2. Assuming your waistband is one-piece, divide the needed change by 2, not by the 4 we used for the waistline, because the waistband pattern piece will be changed at the two side seam areas only. For example, if the waistband needed a 1" increase, 1/2" would be added at each side seam mark. (If your waistband is seamed at the sides, do divide by four cut edges.)

Solutions:

Increase the Waistband

When altering the waistband pattern, start at your *left* and work to your *right* side of the pattern.

1. Draw a line on the waistband pattern at each side seam mark parallel to the ends, as illustrated in Fig. 4-12. The common side seam marking is a square printed on the stitching lines.

2. Align the unnotched edge of the waistband pattern piece along the straight edge of the worksheet. Outline the cutting line of the *left* end of the waistband pattern. Continue to outline the cutting line along the notched edge until you reach the first side seam mark. Transfer the notches marked on the pattern to the worksheet between the end of the waistband and the first side seam mark. (Fig. 4-13)

3. At the side seam mark, **slide** the pattern to the *right* the amount of the needed increase per side seam (in our example, 1/2").

4. Continue to outline the notched edges until you reach the second side seam mark. Again, transfer the notches marked on the pattern to the worksheet between the two side seam marks. (Fig. 4-14)

5. **Slide** the pattern to the *right* the amount of the needed increase per side seam.

6. Outline the remaining cutting line along the notched edge and the remaining end of the pattern. Transfer the remaining notches to the worksheet. (Fig. 4-15)

7. Use the worksheet as the pattern piece for cutting out. Transfer the grainline to the worksheet. Make hash marks for center front and back. (Fig. 4-16)

Decrease the Waistband

Refer to the instructions for increasing the waistband. Instead of sliding the pattern to the right at each side seam, slide it to the *left* to decrease the length of the waistband.

Using the slide technique, the waistband is easily changed without cutting the pattern into many sections. This is a logical way to easily and accurately fit patterns.

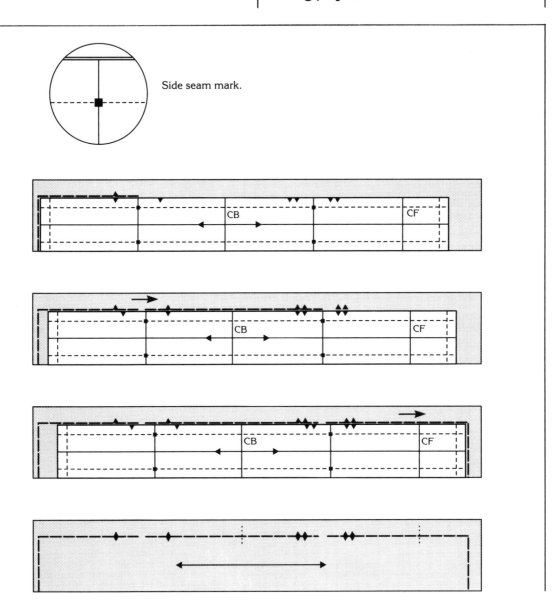

Side seam mark.

CHAPTER 5
HIPLINE SOLUTIONS

How do I:

- *increase the hipline on a skirt?*
- *decrease the hipline on a skirt?*
- *alter the hipline on a one-piece dress?*
- *alter the hipline on a three-piece blazer?*
- *fit a high hip?*

Prepare to Fit

1. Cut out the front and back pattern pieces along the *cutting lines*. Press the pattern tissue pieces with a dry iron.

2. Cut two worksheets (length of wax paper, tissue paper, or a non-woven fabric like Pellon® Tru-Grid®) as long as each pattern piece. It is not necessary that the worksheet be as wide as the pattern since the hipline changes will only be made at the side seam area.

3. Organize your fitting tools:

- red and black permanent marking pens, fine-point
- pins
- tape measure
- French curve
- tape
- tracing wheel

Measure Your Hipline

1. To measure the hipline width, measure around the fullest part of your hipline, keeping the tape measure parallel to the floor.

2. Place a thumb or finger underneath the tape measure to prevent the measurement from being taken too tightly.

3. Measure to the closest 1/2". (Fig. 5-1)

Note From Robbie

Since everything on me, like the national trend, is heading south, the fullest part of my hips is close to the top of my thighs. This is also where I dip in on both sides. If I pull the tape measure tight here, my clothes are apt to accentuate the dips, which I don't want. So I swallow my pride and add liberally to determine my hipline measurement— +2" at least.

4. Take a *second* measurement, the hipline length, measuring the distance between the waist and hip. This measurement will give the hip placement, allowing you to add to or subtract from the pattern at *your* actual hipline. (Fig. 5-2)

N *At the same time as I measure the width around my figure, I simply pick up the loose end of the tape measure to measure the distance between my waist and hip.*

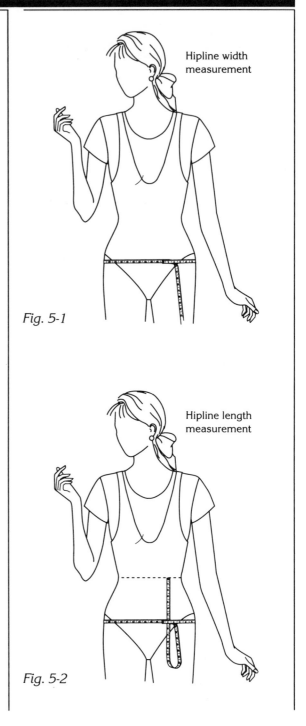

Hipline width measurement

Fig. 5-1

Hipline length measurement

Fig. 5-2

Calculate the Change

1. Compare your hipline measurement to the hipline measurement for your size printed on the pattern back. The difference between the two measurements equals the needed alteration. For, say, a size 12:

Actual Measurement............. 40"

Pattern Envelope .... 36"

Alteration............................ +4"

2. Divide the alteration by 4, the total number of cut edges. In the above example, 1" would be added to each side of the pattern.

Hipline Fitting Challenge #1: "How do I increase the hipline on a skirt?"

Solution:

Note: If your pattern has pockets, see the note on page 41.

1. Place the front pattern piece on top of a worksheet. With the black permanent marker, outline the pattern cutting lines.

2. On the pattern draw the hipline placement perpendicular to the lengthwise grain, using your hipline length measurement for correct placement.

3. At your hipline placement, measure *out* from the hipline *cutting line* the needed increase and mark on the worksheet. Also, measure *out* from the cutting line at the bottom cutting line the same increase amount. (Fig. 5-3)

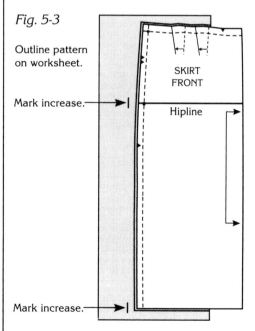

It is important that the hipline increase is added evenly from the hipline to the hemline to keep the design of the skirt in proportion. This is the reason for the amount of the alteration to be added at the bottom cutting line.

Fig. 5-3

Outline pattern on worksheet.

SKIRT FRONT

Mark increase.

Hipline

Mark increase.

4. Place a pin where the waistline and side seam stitching lines cross. **Pivot** the pattern so the *cutting line* meets the increase mark at the hipline. With the red pen, outline the new cutting line between the waistline and hipline. (Fig. 5-4)

5. Keep the pattern pivoted. Move the pivot pin to the stitching line at the hipline. **Pivot** the pattern so the *cutting line* meets the increase mark at the hemline. Outline the new cutting line between the hipline and bottom cutting line. (Fig. 5-5)

6. Tape the pattern to the worksheet, matching the original outline to the old pattern cutting line. Cut out the pattern, following the new outline. (Fig. 5-6)

7. Apply the same techniques to the back piece.

Pivot pattern to meet increase mark at hemline.

Outline new cutting line between hipline and hemline.

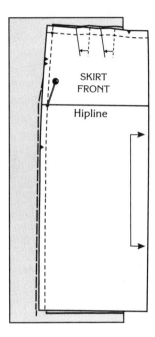

Fig. 5-5

Pivot pattern to meet increase mark at hip.

Outline new cutting line between waistline and hipline.

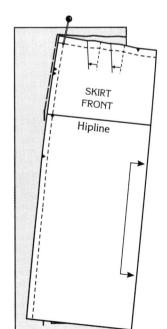

Fig. 5-4

Completed alteration on worksheet.

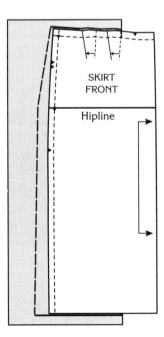

Fig. 5-6

Note: If the skirt pattern has a side pocket pattern piece (Fig. 5-7), pin the pocket section to the skirt pattern, matching the corresponding dots or notches, and treat the pattern as one piece. Place a second layer of wax or tissue paper over the worksheet in the pocket area. Pin together. (Fig. 5-8) Alter the pattern. Trace over the new outline with a tracing wheel. The spokes on the wheel will perforate the two layers of wax paper. Unpin the pattern pieces. Tape the first worksheet to the skirt front pattern and the second worksheet to the pocket pattern. Cut out the pocket, following the new cutting lines. (Fig. 5-9) On the skirt, trace the curved shape of the pocket. Then cut out on the new side seam cutting lines, angling in along the old pocket cutting line to the waistline. (Fig. 5-10)

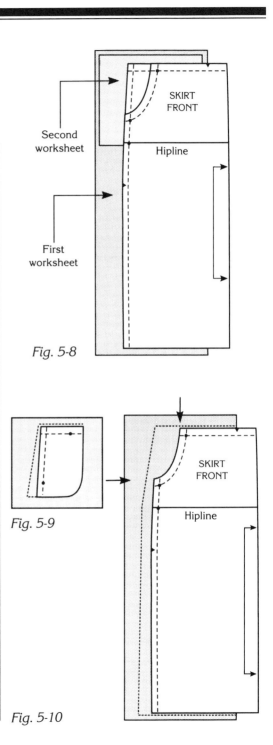

Fig. 5-8

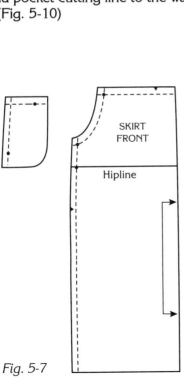

Fig. 5-7

Fig. 5-9

Fig. 5-10

Hipline Fitting Challenge #2: "How do I decrease the hipline on a skirt?"

Solution:

1. Place the front pattern piece on top of a worksheet. With the black permanent marker, outline the pattern cutting line.

2. On the pattern draw the hipline placement perpendicular to the lengthwise grain, using your hipline length measurement for correct placement.

3. At your hipline placement, measure *in* from the hipline *cutting line* the needed decrease and mark on the worksheet. Also, measure *in* from the *cutting line* at the bottom cutting line the same decrease amount.

4. Place a pin where the waistline and side seam stitching lines cross. **Pivot** the pattern so the *cutting line* meets the decrease mark at the hipline. With the red pen, outline the new cutting line between the waistline and hipline. (Fig. 5-11)

5. Keep the pattern pivoted. Move the pivot pin to the stitching line at the hipline. **Pivot** the pattern so the *cutting line* meets the decrease mark at the bottom cutting line. Outline the new cutting line between the hipline and bottom cutting line. (Fig. 5-12)

6. Tape the pattern to the worksheet, matching the original outline and the old pattern cutting line. Cut out the pattern, following the new outline.

7. Apply the same techniques to the back piece.

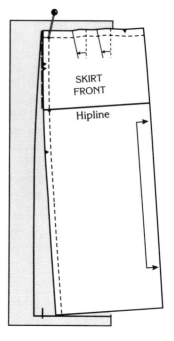

Pivot pattern to meet decrease mark at hip.

Outline new cutting line between waistline and hipline.

SKIRT FRONT

Hipline

Fig. 5-11

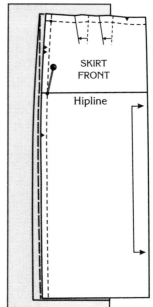

Pivot pattern to meet decrease mark at hemline.

Outline new cutting line between hipline and hemline.

SKIRT FRONT

Hipline

Fig. 5-12

Hipline Fitting Challenge #3: "How do I alter the hipline on a one-piece dress?"

Solution:

Altering the hipline on a one-piece dress pattern is similar to altering the hipline on a skirt. The main difference is that the pivot point has changed to the underarm seam.

1. Place the front pattern piece on top of a worksheet. With the black permanent marker, outline the pattern cutting lines on the worksheet.

2. On the pattern draw a hipline placement perpendicular to the lengthwise grain, using your hipline length measurement.

3. Measure *out* from the hipline *cutting line* the needed increase and mark on the worksheet. Also, measure *out* from the *cutting line* at the bottom cutting line the same increase amount. If decreasing the hipline, measure *in* from the *cutting line* the needed decrease and again at the bottom cutting line. (Fig. 5-13)

4. Place a pin where the underarm and side seam stitching lines cross. **Pivot** the pattern so the *cutting line* meets the increase or decrease mark at the hipline. With the red pen, outline the new cutting line between the underarm and hipline. (Fig. 5-14)

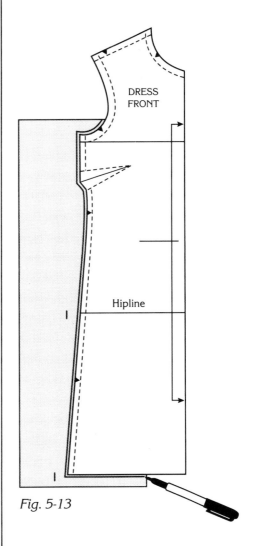

DRESS FRONT

Hipline

Fig. 5-13

5. Keep the pattern pivoted. Move the pivot pin to the stitching line at the hipline. **Pivot** the pattern so the *cutting line* meets the alteration mark at the bottom cutting line. Outline the new cutting line between the hipline and bottom cutting line. (Fig. 5-15)

6. Tape the pattern to the worksheet, matching the original outline to the old pattern cutting lines. Cut out the pattern, following the new outline.

7. Apply the same steps to the back pattern piece.

N N *Notice that the worksheet is placed just under the pattern at the side seam where the changes are being made. It is not necessary to have the worksheet under the entire pattern.*

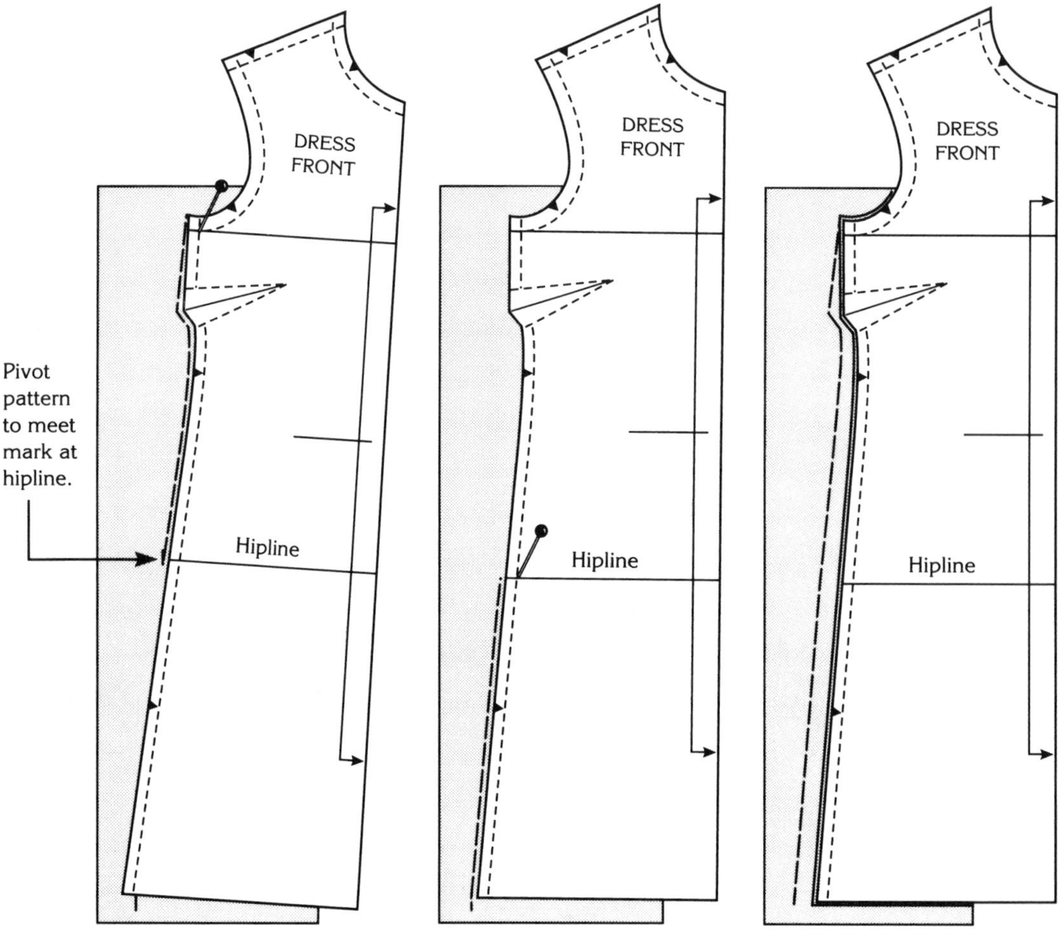

Pivot
pattern
to meet
mark at
hipline.

DRESS
FRONT

Hipline

DRESS
FRONT

Hipline

DRESS
FRONT

Hipline

Fig. 5-14

Fig. 5-15

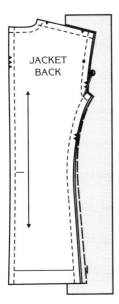
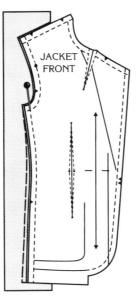

JACKET
BACK

JACKET
FRONT

Fig. 5-16

Hipline Fitting Challenge #4:
"How do I alter the hipline on a three-piece blazer?"

Solution:

Altering a blazer pattern at the hipline is very similar to the preceding changes on a one-piece dress pattern.

1. The front and back pieces are altered, not the side panel. This involves four cut edges, so use the same alteration amount you determined at the beginning of this chapter.

2. Refer to Hipline Fitting Challenge #3 for the steps. Follow the steps, except mark the needed increase (or decrease) only at the hipline. Since the hipline and hemline are practically at the same area, only one mark is needed. (Omit Step 5.) (Fig. 5-16)

Hipline Fitting Challenge #5:
"How do I fit a high hip?"

Solution A: Slightly High Hip

A slightly high hip is commonly found on just one side of the figure. (Fig. 5-17) This alteration is easily made by changing the shape of the side seam. An indicator of a high hip is that the fabric pulls with diagonal stress wrinkles at the higher side, causing an uneven hemline.

N N *It's fairly common to have one high hip along with one square shoulder. The square shoulder will be on the opposite side of the high hip. See Chapter 7 on shoulder alterations for how to solve a square shoulder fitting challenge.*

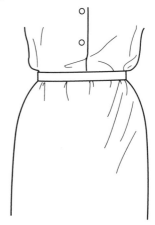

Fig. 5-17

1. Place the front pattern piece on top of a worksheet. With the black permanent marker, outline the pattern cutting lines on the worksheet.

2. Use a French curve to add shape between the waistline and hipline, creating a more predominant curve at the greatest curve of the figure. With the red pen, redraw the side seam cutting line. (Fig. 5-18)

N N *The alteration in Step 2 affects both sides seams, of course, but I find it easier, as well as faster, to cut out both left and right sides of the skirt with the high hip alteration; then I trim off the excess fabric on the lower side. The alternative would be to make a left and right side of the pattern for both front and back—a time-consuming process. KISS!*

3. Make the same changes on the back pattern piece.

4. Pin the pattern to the worksheet, matching the original outline to the old pattern cutting lines. Cut out the pattern, following the new outline.

5. After cutting out the pattern pieces, unpin the pattern from the worksheet. Mark the side of the fabric that is your high hip (left or right). Place the *original pattern* on the side of the skirt that *doesn't* have the high hip. Double-check to be certain you're trimming off the correct side. Trim off the excess fabric added for the high hip. (Fig. 5-19)

6. Repeat this trimming step on the back piece.

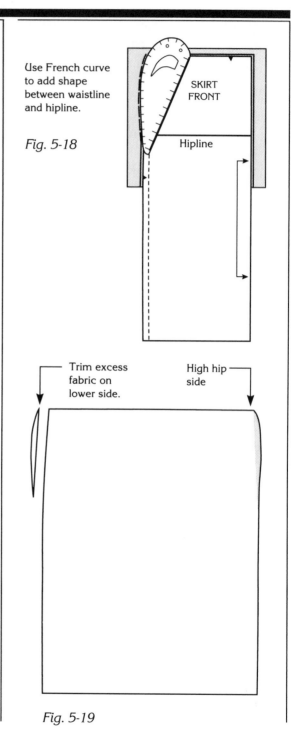

Use French curve to add shape between waistline and hipline.

Fig. 5-18

SKIRT FRONT

Hipline

Trim excess fabric on lower side.

High hip side

Fig. 5-19

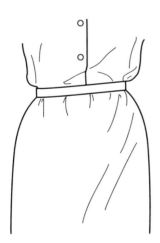

If you have a high hip, avoid patterned fabric such as plaids and stripes that would accentuate the changes we've made.

Note From Robbie

After 20 years of back problems, I recently discovered one leg is 1" longer than the other. In raising the shoe on my short side, my back pain disappeared, but so did my high hip wrinkles. Sometimes you should alter your body instead of the pattern.

Solution B: Extremely High Hip

If one side of the figure has an extreme high hip, not only width at the side seams but extra length at the top of the waistline is needed. It is difficult to measure the difference in inches between a low hip and a high hip. To simplify the alteration, change the pattern in 1/4" increments. Usually 1/4" added at the high hip side seam and waistline will give sufficient room (1/4" side seam gives 1/2" total width). But if you feel

Fig. 5-20

that a total of 1" at the side seam would be more in proportion with your figure, please add accordingly.

I realize that this is an ambiguous amount to add. No doubt, fine-tuning this alteration in the fitting step will be needed. Keep in mind that you can always take away fabric during the fitting step, but you can't add more.

1. Place the front pattern piece on top of a worksheet. With the black permanent marker, outline the pattern cutting lines on the worksheet. The worksheet needs to be wider than the pattern, but only needs to cover the length between the waist and hip.

2. Working 3" to 4" below the waistline on the side seam (the high hip area), measure *out* 1/4" from the *cutting line*. Also, measure *up* from the end of the *waistline cutting line* the 1/4". Make marks for both. (Fig. 5-21)

3. Place a pin at the center front waistline in the stitching line. **Pivot** the pattern so the *cutting line* meets the *waistline* increase mark. With the red pen, outline the new waistline cutting line. (Fig. 5-22)

4. Keep the pattern pivoted. Move the pivot pin to the stitching lines where waistline and side seam cross. **Pivot** the pattern to meet the high hip increase mark. Outline the new cutting line between the waistline and high hip. (Fig. 5-23)

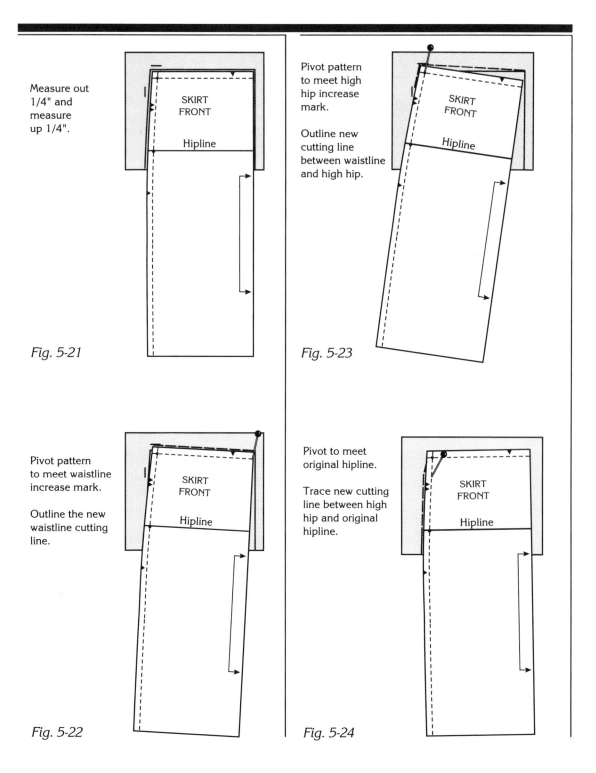

Measure out 1/4" and measure up 1/4".

SKIRT FRONT

Hipline

Fig. 5-21

Pivot pattern to meet high hip increase mark.

Outline new cutting line between waistline and high hip.

SKIRT FRONT

Hipline

Fig. 5-23

Pivot pattern to meet waistline increase mark.

Outline the new waistline cutting line.

SKIRT FRONT

Hipline

Fig. 5-22

Pivot to meet original hipline.

Trace new cutting line between high hip and original hipline.

SKIRT FRONT

Hipline

Fig. 5-24

5. Keep the pattern pivoted. Move the pivot pin to the stitching line at the high hip area. **Pivot** the pattern so the *cutting line* meets the original hipline. Trace the new cutting line between the high and original hipline. (Fig. 5-24)

6. Apply the same steps to the back pattern piece.

7. Pin the pattern to the worksheet, matching the original outline to the old pattern cutting lines. Cut out the pattern, following the new outline. (Fig. 5-25)

8. After cutting out the pattern pieces, unpin the worksheet from the pattern. On the fabric, mark the side that is your high hip (left or right). Place the original pattern on the side of the skirt that *doesn't* have the high hip. Double-check to be certain you're trimming off the correct side. Cut off the excess fabric at the waistline and side seam added for the high hip. (Fig. 5-26) Repeat this trimming on the back piece.

9. Machine baste the side seams of the skirt together. Check the fit by pinning the skirt to your slip at the center front and center back. Check the fit at the high hip side. If too much fullness and/or length has been added to the pattern, note the changes on the pattern piece for future reference, and make the changes on the skirt itself.

N N *If a regular hipline increase is also needed, simply pivot from the high hipline to the hipline increase mark. Chapter 9 covers how to combine alterations.*

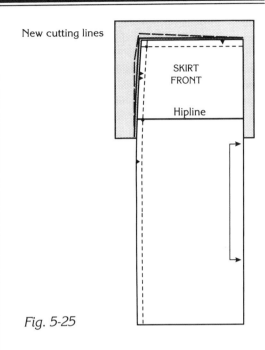

Fig. 5-25

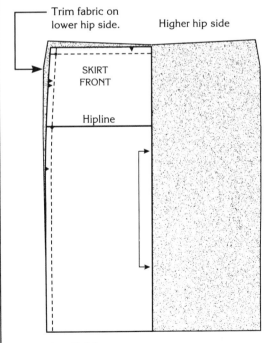

Fig. 5-26

Solution C: High Full Hips at Both Sides of Figure

The term "high hip" usually refers to one side higher than the other. But if a figure is full above the hips and below the waist at the side seams, we also call it high hips. Refer to one of the preceding alterations. Follow the instructions until the step that refers to trimming off the excess fabric for the lower hip side. Obviously, this step isn't necessary, since you need it for both sides.

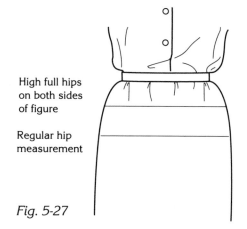

High full hips on both sides of figure

Regular hip measurement

Fig. 5-27

N N *Learn to alter for your body's special requirements. You may have a larger than normal ribcage or high full hips that require an additional measurement. But the same principle applies: once you know what to do on a classic-style pattern, you can automatically apply the same alteration to any pattern from the same company, without further measurement.*

CHAPTER 6

SLEEVE SOLUTIONS

How do I:

- *increase the width of a short sleeve?*
- *increase the width of a long sleeve?*
- *increase a two-piece sleeve, as found in a blazer pattern?*
- *lengthen or shorten a sleeve?*
- *pivot more than 1" per cut edge?*

Prepare to Fit

1. Cut out the sleeve pattern piece along the *cutting lines*. Press the pattern tissue piece with a dry iron.

2. Cut a worksheet (length of wax paper, tissue paper, or a non-woven fabric like Pellon's® Tru-Grid®) as long and as wide as the pattern piece.

3. Organize your fitting tools:

- red and black permanent marking pens, fine-point
- pins
- tape measure
- ruler
- tape
- tracing wheel (for wax paper)

Measure Your Upper Arm

The only way to determine if you need to add width to the sleeve is to measure your arm, measure the actual pattern, and then compare the difference. It is not possible to compare your arm measurement to a measurement on the back of the pattern envelope, since the pattern companies do not give the sleeve width.

1. Measure the fullest part of your arm between the shoulder and elbow, measuring with a thumb or finger underneath the tape measure. Have someone take this measurement for you, as it is extremely difficult to do by yourself.

2. Measure to the closest 1/2". (Fig. 6-1)

3. Add 2" to the arm measurement. This 2" is the *minimum ease* for a basic set-in sleeve.

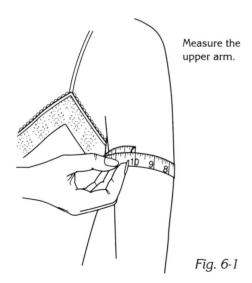

Measure the upper arm.

Fig. 6-1

Note: Be sure to use a classic-style blouse or dress pattern with a basic set-in sleeve when first using these alteration techniques. Since the arm width is not given on the pattern envelope, I've used the 2" ease of a basic set-in sleeve. On future projects, measuring and checking of the sleeve will not be necessary. No matter what the style, just add to that sleeve pattern whatever measurement you used for this basic set-in sleeve.

Calculate the Change

1. Measure the pattern by placing the tape measure across the width of the sleeve pattern at the underarm, measuring from *stitching line to stitching line*. (Fig. 6-2)

2. Subtract the pattern measurement from your upper arm measurement (which includes the 2" of ease).

Arm Measurement + 2" ease 16"

Pattern Measurement...... 14-1/2"

Alteration .... +1-1/2"

3. Divide the increase by 2, the number of cut edges. (For example, if 1-1/2" were needed, 3/4" would be added at each cut edge of the sleeve.)

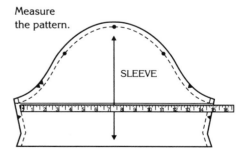

Measure the pattern.

SLEEVE

Fig. 6-2

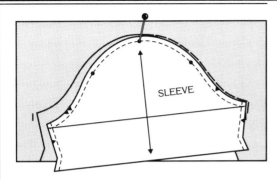

Pivot pattern to meet one increase mark.
Outline half of sleeve cap and 1" of side seam.

Fig. 6-3

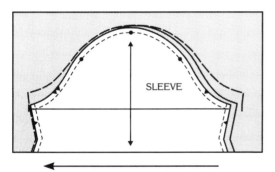

Slide pattern to meet increase.
Outline new side seam.

Fig. 6-4

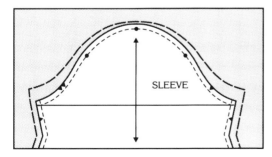

Completed alteration for sleeve increase.

Fig. 6-5

 If you need to pivot more than 1" per cut edge, please also read about adding Extra Extensions on page 60.

Sleeve Fitting Challenge #1: "How do I increase the width of a short sleeve?"

Solution:

1. Place the sleeve piece on top of a worksheet. With the black permanent marker, outline the pattern cutting lines.

2. Measure *out* from both sides of the side seam *cutting lines* the needed increase (in the example, 3/4"). Place marks on the worksheet at the underarm.

3. Place a pin at the large dot at the cap of the sleeve. **Pivot** the pattern so that the *cutting line* meets one increase mark. With the red pen, outline one half of the sleeve, following the cutting line, and 1" of the side seam. *Do not draw the entire side seam.* (Fig. 6-3)

4. Place the sleeve in the original position and **pivot** the pattern so the other *cutting line* meets the second increase mark. Outline the other half of the sleeve cap, following the cutting line and 1" of the side seam.

5. To finish the sleeve, **slide** the pattern horizontally along the hemline, until it meets the increase line drawn in Step 4. Outline the new side seam. Repeat on the other side. (Fig. 6-4)

6. Tape the pattern to the worksheet, matching the original outline to the old pattern cutting lines. Cut out the pattern, following the new outline. (Fig. 6-5)

Sleeve Fitting Challenge #2: "How do I increase the width of a long sleeve?"

Solution:

1. Place the sleeve piece on top of a worksheet. With the black permanent marker, outline the pattern cutting lines on the worksheet.

2. Measure *out* from both sides of the side seam *cutting lines* the needed increase (in the example, 3/4"). Place marks on the worksheet at the underarm parallel to the side seam cutting line.

3. Place a pin at the large dot at the cap of the sleeve. **Pivot** the pattern so that the *cutting line* meets one increase mark. With the red pen, outline one half of the sleeve cap, following the cutting line, and 1" of the side seam. Do not draw the entire side seam. (Fig. 6-6)

4. Keep the pattern pivoted and transfer the pin to the underarm where the cap and the side seam stitching lines cross.

5. **Pivot** the pattern so the *cutting line* at the bottom of the sleeve meets the *cutting line* on the worksheet. Outline the new sleeve seam, which gradually tapers to the original line at the hem. (Fig. 6-7)

6. Repeat Steps 3-5 on the other side of the long sleeve.

7. Tape the pattern to the worksheet, matching the original outline to the old pattern cutting lines. Cut out the pattern, following the new outline.

Pivot pattern to meet one increase mark. Outline half of sleeve cap and 1" of side seam.

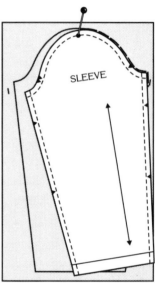

Fig. 6-6

Pivot pattern so cutting line at bottom meets cutting line on worksheet. Outline new side seam.

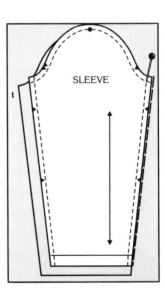

Fig. 6-7

Sleeve Fitting Challenge #3: "How do I increase a two-piece sleeve, as found in a blazer pattern?"

Solution:

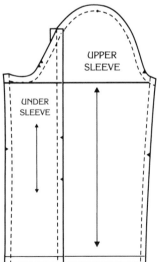

Earlier, I suggested that you try alterations first on classic-style patterns. Once you know how much to add or subtract on classic styles, you can transfer the same alterations to more stylized patterns without remeasuring. In other words, once you determine your "recipe" of changes, the same recipe can be applied to other styles within the same pattern size. For example, if you added to the sleeve pattern on a basic set-in sleeve, add the same amount to this two-piece blazer sleeve.

With two pattern pieces for one garment part, we usually stack seams and proceed as if the two were one pattern piece. But in this instance, we will add width only to the upper sleeve. The under sleeve will only be changed in the length to match the widened upper sleeve. As with sleeves, this alteration does not change the sleeve cap, so the sleeve still fits perfectly into the armhole of the jacket.

1. Pin the sleeve pattern pieces together at the underarm seam, stacking the stitching lines.

2. Perpendicular to the grainline, extend a line from the underarm stitching line of the under sleeve to the upper sleeve. Unpin the two sleeve pattern pieces. (Fig. 6-9)

Fig. 6-8

UPPER SLEEVE

UNDER SLEEVE

Pin sleeve patterns together. Draw a line from underarm stitching line of upper sleeve to under sleeve.

Fig. 6-9

Outline upper sleeve
pattern piece.

Measure out increase
on both sides of
pattern.

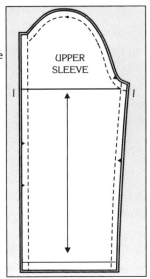

Fig. 6-10

Pivot pattern
to meet one
increase mark.

Outline new
cutting line
between dot
and increase
mark.

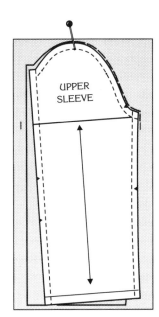

Fig. 6-11

Upper Sleeve

3. Place a worksheet under the upper pattern only. With the black pen, outline the pattern on the worksheet.

4. Measure *out* the needed increase on both sides of the sleeve at the under-arm, parallel to the side seam *cutting line*. Place marks on the worksheet. (Fig. 6-10)

5. Place a pin at the sleeve cap dot. **Pivot** the sleeve so the *cutting line* meets one increase mark. With the red pen, outline the new cutting line be-tween the cap and the increase mark. (Fig. 6-11)

6. Keep the pattern in the pivoted po-sition. Move the pin from the cap to the underarm where the cap and side seam stitching lines cross. **Pivot** the pattern to meet the original outline at the bot-tom of the sleeve.

7. Outline the remaining side seam. (Fig. 6-12)

8. Repeat Steps 5-7 on the other side of the sleeve.

9. Tape the pattern to the worksheet, matching the original outline to the old pattern cutting lines. Cut out the pat-tern, following the new outline. (Fig. 6-13)

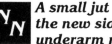 *A small jut may be noticed at the new side seam near the underarm mark. Simply straighten the cutting line with a ruler.*

Pivot pattern
to meet original
outline at sleeve
bottom.

Outline new
side seam.

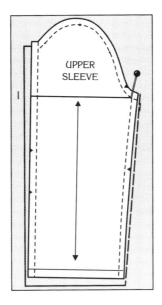

Fig. 6-12

Completed
alteration
on worksheet

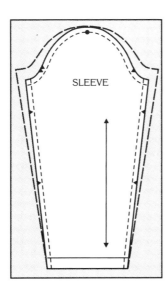

Fig. 6-13

Under Sleeve

To match the alterations on the upper sleeve, the under sleeve must be lengthened.

10. On the upper sleeve at the underarm seam, measure the distance between the original outline and the altered sleeve. Record the amount. (Fig. 6-14)

11. With the black pen, outline the under sleeve on a worksheet. Extend the grainline. Draw this extended grainline on the worksheet. From the underarm seam, measure *up* the amount determined in Step 10. Mark on the worksheet. (Fig. 6-15)

12. **Slide** the pattern *up*, following the grainline, to meet the mark, keeping the grainline straight.

13. With the red pen, trace the raised underarm section and 1" of each side.

14. Tape the pattern to the worksheet, matching the original outline to the old pattern cutting line. Cut out the pattern, following the new outline.

 Visually, the altered pattern pieces may appear higher and more binding at the underarm. But it is an illusion. If you match the new cutting lines to the original cutting lines, you'll find that the armhole is the same size, yet the width of the arm is larger. This alteration is accomplished without slashing the pattern and spreading it apart, allowing the grainline to remain straight and the cutting lines, even. Again and again, Pivot and Slide Techniques save time for the busy woman.

Measure distance between original outline and new cutting line.

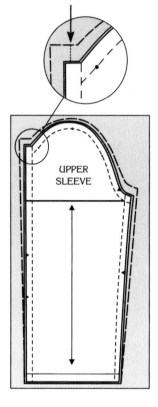

UPPER SLEEVE

Fig. 6-14

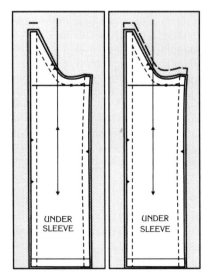

UNDER SLEEVE

UNDER SLEEVE

Fig. 6-15

Sleeve Fitting Challenge #4: "How do I lengthen or shorten a sleeve?"

Measure the Sleeve Length

1. Have someone feel for the knob at the end of your shoulder and keep a finger there. (Depending on your body, it may help to raise your elbow shoulder-high.)

2. Place your hand on your hip. Have your friend measure from the shoulder knob over the elbow to your wrist bone. (Measuring with your arm bent builds in ease for your sleeve.) (Fig. 6-16)

3. Pin the cuff piece to the sleeve pattern, stacking the stitching lines. Measure the sleeve length from the stitching line at the cap to the bottom stitching line of the cuff. *Note:* For straight sleeves without cuffs, simply measure the sleeve length itself between the cap and wrist stitching lines. For tapered sleeves without cuffs, see Chapter 9, Figs. 9-10 and 9-11.

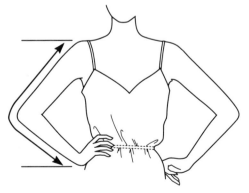

Fig. 6-16

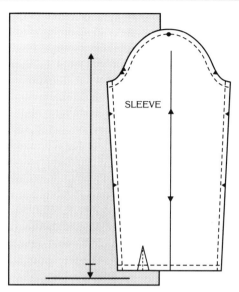

Trace lower edge of sleeve. Measure increase up from lower cutting edge.

Fig. 6-17

To lengthen sleeve, slide pattern up to meet increase mark.

Outline pattern.

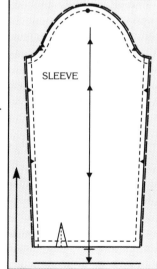

Fig. 6-18

4. Subtract the pattern measurement from your measurement to determine how much you need to lengthen or shorten the pattern.

Solution:

1. Place the sleeve on top of a worksheet. With the black pen, outline *only* the lower edge cutting line.

2. Extend the grainline on the pattern to the lower edge and draw this extended grainline on the worksheet. If you are using wax paper for a worksheet, trace the grainline on the pattern with a tracing wheel. The marks will automatically transfer to the wax paper.

3. To lengthen the pattern, measure *up* on the worksheet from the lower edge cutting line the needed amount and mark. (To shorten the pattern, measure *down* the amount needed to subtract from the length.) (Fig. 6-17)

4. Place the pattern on the original lower edge outline. **Slide** the pattern *up*, following the grainline, until the pattern meets the lengthening mark. (Fig. 6-18) (To shorten, **slide** the pattern *down*.)

5. With the red pen, outline the top and sides of the pattern, connecting the bottom sides to the old lower edge cutting line.

6. Tape the pattern to the worksheet, matching the outline drawn in Step 5. If the sleeve was shortened, fold up the original pattern so the shorter outline can be seen. Cut out the pattern, following the new outline. (Fig. 6-19)

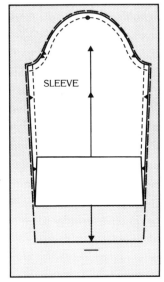

To shorten sleeve, slide pattern down to meet decrease mark.

Outline pattern.

Fold pattern tissue so shorter hemline is visible.

SLEEVE

Fig. 6-19

N *At first this may seem backwards, sliding up to lengthen, down to shorten. If you can't visualize it, make a small paper model for yourself and follow the steps. You'll soon see that it works.*

When You Need to Pivot More Than 1"

As with many alteration methods, **Pivot and Slide Techniques** have a few limitations. The main limitation with this method is that the bustline and sleeve pivot amount *cannot exceed 1" per side seam* (a total increase of 4" for the bustline or a 2" increase for sleeves). Pivoting over 1" per side seam at either the bustline or sleeve raises the armhole too high.

If you are now using a much smaller size of pattern because of your Front Width Measurement or if you are full-busted, you will probably need to add more than 1" per side seam at the bustline and sleeve. If you need more than 1" added per side seam in these areas, consider adding Extra Extensions or using a princess-style pattern (see Chapter 10).

N *The limit of pivoting 1" per side seam only refers to the bustline and sleeve. The hipline and waistline can be increased by any amount—no limit.*

Extra Extensions

Extra Extensions are sections added at the underarm of the bodice and sleeve patterns to give the needed increase beyond pivoting. These sections are added in combination with pivoting techniques and are made by sliding the pattern sidewards.

Calculate the Extra Extensions

When adding many inches to the pattern at the bustline and sleeve, first work with the sleeve. Subtract the maximum amount allowed for sleeve pivoting (2") from your needed alteration amount. The remainder will become Extra Extensions.

Sleeve Alteration:

For example, suppose you need 4" added to your sleeve.

Needed Sleeve Increase: 4"

Maximum Pivoting at Sleeve: 2" (1" per side seam)

Needed Extra Extensions*: +2" (1" per side seam)

*The **same** Extra Extensions must be added to the bustline area so the sleeve armholes will match the bodice armholes. Use this Extra Extension amount to calculate the needed bustline increase.

Bustline Alteration:

Suppose you also need 5" added to your bust. Remember, you *must* apply the same Extra Extensions to both the sleeve and bustline. In the example above, that was 2", which becomes 1" *per side seam* (4" total). To find out how much is left to be pivoted, subtract the Extra Extensions amount from your needed bustline alteration amount.

Needed Bustline Increase: 5"

Needed Extra Extension: 4" (1" per side side, determined in Sleeve Alteration above)

Needed Pivoting: +1" (1/4" per side seam)

Since this procedure may be new, let me summarize:

If you need more than:

- 4" on the bustline or
- 2" on the sleeve

you must pivot and you must add Extra Extensions.

Step 1. Calculate your needed sleeve alteration. Subtract maximum pivot amount (2"). Remainder equals Extra Extension amount. (This Extra Extension amount must also be added to bustline.) Divide by 2 for amount per side seam.

Step 2. Calculate your needed bustline alteration. Subtract Extra Extension from needed alteration. Remainder equals amount to be pivoted. Divide by 4 for amount per side seam.

Change the Pattern with Pivoting and Extra Extensions

1. Put the sleeve and bodice front patterns on worksheets. **Pivot** the patterns first. In the example, pivot 1" per side seam at the sleeve and 1/4" per side seam for the bustline.

2. Add Extra Extensions at the side seams of the sleeve. On the worksheet, measure out the 1" section from the *new* cutting line at the underarm. **Slide** the pattern to the increase mark and trace the extension from the end of the pivot increase to the corner. On short sleeves, extend the Extra Extensions the entire length of the side seam. (Fig. 6-20)

On long sleeves, the Extra Extensions taper to the elbow area (the middle of the underarm seam).

3. Add an Extra Extension at the side seam of the bodice front. On the worksheet, measure out the 1" section from the *new* cutting line at the underarm. Taper the extension to the cutting line at the waistline. (Fig. 6-21)

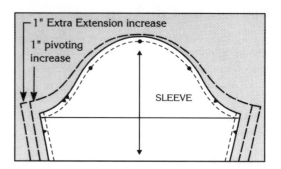

Fig. 6-20

N N *Use Extra Extensions only in combination with pivoting. Without pivoting, an extension does not give the room needed to raise your arm—the garment would be extremely constricting.*

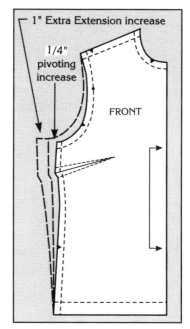

Fig. 6-21

CHAPTER 7

SHOULDER AND BACK SOLUTIONS

How do I:

- *shorten shoulder width?*
- *broaden the shoulders?*
- *fit sloping shoulders?*
- *fit one lower shoulder?*
- *fit square shoulders?*
- *prevent tightness across the back?*

Has this common sewing experience happened to you? You buy a pattern to fit your bust measurement, spend hours sewing, and end up unhappy with the droopy fit around the neck, shoulders, and armholes. You are not alone—but now you have the Front Width Measurement, your key to a perfect fit.

Now you have purchased a smaller pattern size according to your Front Width Measurement. Congratulations— many of your alteration challenges are over!

As you have read in earlier chapters, it is easy to change the bust, waist, hip, or sleeve widths of the pattern when the shape of the shoulders, armhole, and neckline fit your body. Still, even though many of your major fitting challenges are solved by buying the pattern to fit your upper body, you may need to fine-tune the fit of the shoulders in width and the fit across your back.

Prepare to Fit

1. Cut out the front and back pattern pieces along the *cutting lines*. Press the pattern tissue pieces with a dry iron.

2. Cut two worksheets (lengths of wax paper, tissue paper, or a non-woven fabric like Pellon's® Tru-Grid®) as long as each pattern piece.

3. Organize your fitting tools:

- red and black permanent marking pens, fine-point
- pins
- tape measure
- tape
- Tru-Grid® (optional)
- yardstick (optional)

(Don't) Measure Your Shoulders

The width of the shoulder that the designer intended for the pattern you chose is difficult to measure. Study the picture on your pattern. Is it a dropped shoulder? Should it end at the knob where your shoulder joins your arm? Since the shoulder is a style feature and we can only guess at the designer's intentions, it is impossible to measure the shoulder width accurately for each pattern.

For example, Fig. 7-1 shows the shoulder widths of a jacket, blouse, and vest. All are correct, yet all vary. You can see that measuring your body will not be of value.

Calculate the Change

If the Front Width Measurement indicated that you have been buying the correct size pattern already and if you know from experience that your garments are consistently too narrow or too wide at the shoulders, use the methods below to change your patterns. Challenge #1 is for narrow shoulders; #2, for wide shoulders.

If, on the other hand, your Front Width Measurement revealed that you should be buying a smaller size pattern and if you've always thought you had narrow shoulders, you may find that your droopy shoulder problem has disappeared. Still, you may not trust this new approach until you've tried it. If so, see Challenge #1, Method B.

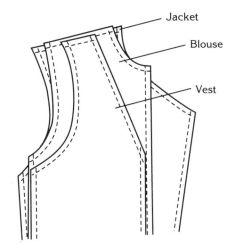

Jacket

Blouse

Vest

Fig. 7-1

Shoulder Fitting Challenge #1: "I have narrow shoulders. How do I shorten the shoulder width on patterns?" (Fig. 7-2)

To achieve the correct shoulder fit, use one of the following techniques:

Method A: Use a Fitting Formula

If the Front Width Measurement indicated that you should purchase a pattern the same size you've been using, and the shoulders are still too broad, a 1/4" or 1/2" alteration will fit your needs.

Use these tested amounts to quickly determine how much to change the pattern.

Slightly Narrow Shoulders: Subtract 1/4"

Very Narrow Shoulders: Subtract 1/2"

See Solution below for procedures.

Narrow shoulders

Fig. 7-2

N N *A 1/4" or 1/2" decrease may not seem like a major change, but the average shoulder width is only 5". Subtracting 1/2" results in reducing the shoulder width by 10%—that's quite a change.*

Method B: Make a Quick Trial Garment

If you have purchased a smaller pattern size using the Front Width Measurement, the fitting challenge of the shoulders being too wide may have been eliminated. If you think the shoulders of the pattern may still need to be narrower, consider making a quick trial garment out of Tru-Grid® (a gridded

non-woven fabric designed specifically for trial garments).

N N *I usually do not recommend making a trial garment to test an alteration, but in the case of the shoulder, where accurately measuring the shoulder width is difficult, this many be a worthwhile step.*

Make the trial garment as simple as possible. Tru-Grid® (or a comparable product) makes an excellent quick trial garment. (Fig. 7-3) Cut out and sew together the front and back pattern pieces at the shoulder and side seams, sewing in the darts. Set in *one* sleeve. Trim away the 5/8" seam allowance at the neckline. Try on and pin the garment closed.

When checking the fit of the trial garment, place a pin on the shoulder seam of the set-in sleeve side where you think the armhole seam should fall. Have a friend help you. Then measure the distance between the pin and the armhole seam. That's how much you need to remove. (Usually no more than 3/4" will be taken out of the shoulder. As in Method A, 1/4" and 1/2" is the more common alteration.

See below for removing this amount from your pattern.

Solution:

To narrow the shoulder width, a combination of **Pivoting and Sliding Techniques** are used.

1. Place the front pattern piece on top of a worksheet. With the black permanent marker, outline the cutting lines on the worksheet.

2. Measure *in* from the shoulder *cutting line* the decrease amount. Mark on the worksheet.

3. Place the pattern on top of the worksheet, matching the outline. **Slide** the pattern so the shoulder *cutting line* meets the decrease mark. (Fig. 7-4)

4. Place a pin where the shoulder and armhole stitching lines cross. **Pivot** the pattern so the *cutting line* meets the original outline at the underarm.

5. With the red pen, outline the new armhole cutting line. (Fig. 7-5)

6. Tape the pattern to the worksheet, matching the original outline to the pattern cutting lines. Fold the pattern out of

Tru-Grid trial garment

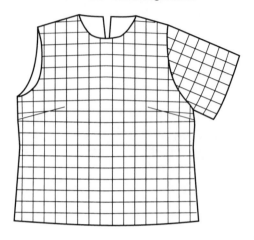

Sew shoulder and side seams. Set in one sleeve. Trim away neckline seam allowance.

Fig. 7-3

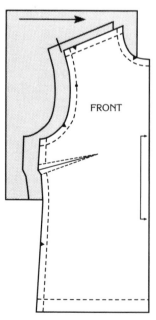

Outline pattern. Measure decrease in from shoulder line.

Slide pattern so shoulder cutting line meets decrease mark.

FRONT

Fig. 7-4

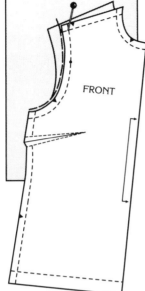

Pivot pattern
to meet original
outline at underarm.

Trace new armhole.

FRONT

Fig. 7-5

the way, so the new cutting lines are visible. Cut out the pattern, following the new outline. (Fig. 7-6)

7. Repeat on the back piece.

Note that the altered armhole is the same size as the armhole on the original pattern. It may appear slightly higher, but it will fit correctly with the sleeve.

Shoulder Fitting Challenge #2: "How do I broaden the shoulders?"

Having shoulders that are broader than the pattern is not as common of a fitting challenge as having narrow shoulders. Broad shoulders create stress wrinkles at the sleeve cap, both on the front and the back. (Fig. 7-7) These wrinkles can be avoided by widening the shoulders, using **Pivot and Slide Techniques**.

Fold pattern
so new cutting
line is visible.

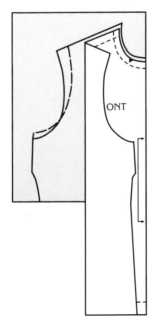

ONT

Fig. 7-6

Broad
shoulders

Fig. 7-7

To achieve the correct shoulder fit, use one of the following methods:

Method A: Use a Fitting Formula

If the Front Width Measurement indicated that you should purchase a pattern the same size you've been using and the shoulders are still too broad, a 1/4" or 1/2" alteration will fit your needs.

Use these tested amounts to determine quickly how much to change the pattern.

Slightly Broad Shoulders: Add 1/4"

Very Broad Shoulders: Add 1/2"

See Solution below for procedures.

Method B: Make a Quick Trial Garment

Make a quick trial garment (refer to the section on decreasing the shoulder width on page 65). See Solution on the next page for adding to your pattern as much as you need.

Solution:

1. Place a worksheet under the pattern. Outline the cutting lines on the worksheet with the black permanent marking pen.

2. Measure *out* from the shoulder *cutting line* on the worksheet the increase amount determined from Method A or Method B. (Fig. 7-8)

3. **Slide** the pattern so the shoulder *cutting line* meets the increase mark.

4. With the red pen, outline the wider shoulder cutting line. (Fig. 7-9)

5. Place a pin where the shoulder and armhole stitching lines cross. **Pivot** the pattern so the *cutting line* meets the original outline at the underarm. Outline the new armhole cutting line. (Fig. 7-10)

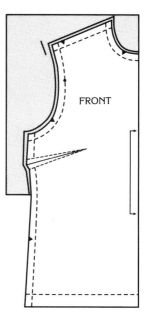

Outline pattern. Measure increase out from shoulder line.

Slide pattern so shoulder cutting line meets increase mark.

FRONT

Fig. 7-8

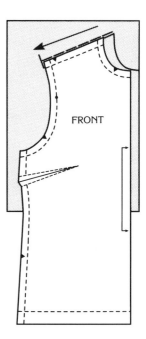

Slide pattern to meet increase mark.

Outline new shoulder cutting line.

FRONT

Fig. 7-9

Pivot pattern to meet original outline at underarm.

Trace new armhole cutting line.

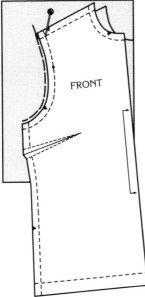

FRONT

Fig. 7-10

Completed broad shoulder change on worksheet

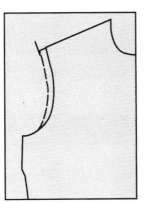

Fig. 7-11

6. Tape the pattern to the worksheet. Fold any part of the pattern that overlaps the new cutting line out of the way. Cut out the pattern, following the new outline. (Fig. 7-11)

7. Repeat on the back pattern piece.

This method adds a little to your Front Width Measurement too, but it isn't enough to affect the final look of your garment.

 The great advantage of using Pivot and Slide Techniques is that the original pattern shape is maintained. Here again, the shoulder width has been extended while keeping the armhole the same size and shape.

Shoulder Fitting Challenge #3: "How do I fit a pattern to sloping shoulders?"

If you have sloping shoulders, your clothes will often bind at the underarm. You may also see wrinkles form at the underarm. (Fig. 7-12)

The front and back pattern pieces can easily be changed to fit your body shape by using simple **pivoting** techniques.

Calculate the Change

Accurate body measurements for all shoulder alterations are difficult to take. Your cue that you have sloping shoulders and need to change your pattern is that on most of your garments, wrinkles form at the underarm and/or the bodice binds at the underarm.

As with the narrow and broad shoulder alterations, use this simple fitting formula when determining the alteration amounts.

Slightly Sloping Shoulders: Subtract 1/4"

Very Sloping Shoulders: Subtract 1/2"

If you are not sure how much your shoulders slope, hold a yardstick parallel to the floor at your neck and look in the mirror. Is the angle between the edge of the yardstick and your shoulders like a ski ramp? You have very sloping shoulders.

Solution:

1. Place a worksheet under the front pattern piece. Outline the pattern cutting lines on the worksheet, using the black permanent marking pen.

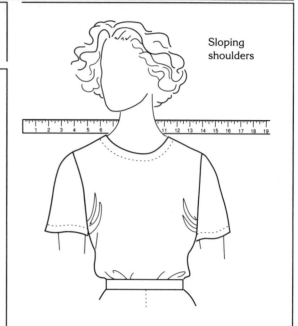

Sloping shoulders

Fig. 7-12

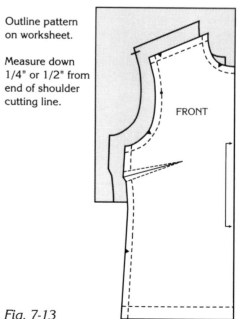

Outline pattern on worksheet.

Measure down 1/4" or 1/2" from end of shoulder cutting line.

FRONT

Fig. 7-13

Pivot pattern
to meet
decrease mark.

Outline new
shoulder
cutting line.

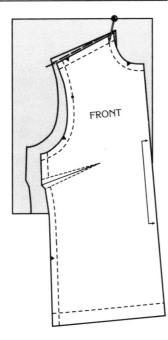

FRONT

Fig. 7-14

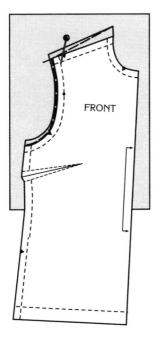

FRONT

Fig. 7-15

2. Measure *down* 1/4" or 1/2" from the end of the shoulder *cutting line.* Mark on the worksheet. (Fig. 7-13)

3. Place a pin where the neckline and shoulder stitching lines cross. **Pivot** the pattern until the pattern *cutting line* meets the decrease mark.

4. With the red pen, outline the new shoulder cutting line on the worksheet. (Fig. 7-14)

5. Keep the pattern pivoted. Place a pivot pin where the shoulder and armhole stitching lines cross. **Pivot** the pattern so the *cutting line* meets the original outline at the underarm. Trace the new armhole cutting line. (Fig. 7-15)

6. Tape the pattern to the worksheet, matching the original outline marks. Fold any part of the pattern that overlaps the new cutting line out of the way. Cut out the pattern, following the new outline. (Fig. 7-16)

7. Repeat on the back pattern piece. The new pattern armhole now slopes at a greater angle to match your body shape, preventing the garment from binding at the underarms, as well as eliminating the wrinkles caused by sloping shoulders.

Completed
alteration
on worksheet.

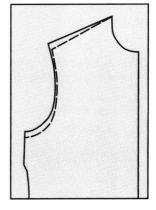

Fig. 7-16

Note From Robbie

Isn't it funny how you can sew happily for years without realizing you have a "problem"? I didn't know I had sloping shoulders until I took a fit class. The teacher showed me how shoulder pads eliminated my wrinkles and raised my shoulder level. Fine. Wonderful. But I can't be the only woman in the world who hates wearing 17" of shoulder pads, by the time you stack up coat, blazer, sweater, blouse. It makes me feel like a football player. Now, on blouses, instead of wearing shoulder pads, I use Nancy's pivoting technique to eliminate the wrinkles caused by my sloping shoulders. No more shoulder pads on everyday wear. I'm back to happy sewing.

Shoulder Fitting Challenge #4: "I have one shoulder lower than the other. How do I change for that one side?"

Solution:

It is fairly common to have one shoulder lower than the other. If this is your fitting challenge:

1. Cut the pattern out of your fabric without making the sloping shoulder alteration.

2. Unpin the pattern pieces from the front and back fabric pieces.

3. Make the sloping shoulder changes on a worksheet (refer to the steps in Challenge #3 for sloping shoulder solution). Cut out the worksheet from Fig. 7-16.

4. Place the worksheet *only* on the side of the fabric that corresponds to the

One sloping shoulder

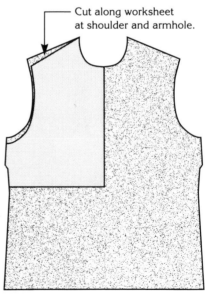

Cut along worksheet at shoulder and armhole.

Front piece cut from fabric

Fig. 7-17

sloping shoulder. Double-check before you cut.

5. Recut *both* the front and the back of the garment, using the worksheet as a cutting guide. (Fig. 7-17)

Note From Robbie

Please see my comment on page 47 about altering your body vs. altering the pattern.

Shoulder Fitting Challenge #5: "How do I fit a pattern to my square shoulders?"

Calculate the Change

If you have square shoulders, the garment rides up at the neckline, creating bias stress wrinkles at the shoulders and causing the neckline to feel unfitted or too large (Fig. 7-18). Your best cue as to whether you should make pattern changes for square shoulders is the ill-fit of an existing garment.

As with the other shoulder changes in this chapter, it is difficult to measure how much to change the pattern. KISS—keep it simple and use the following Fitting Formula:

Slightly Square Shoulders: Add 1/4"

Very Square Shoulders: Add 1/2"

Solution:

1. Place a worksheet under the front pattern piece. With the black permanent marker, outline the pattern cutting lines on the worksheet.

2. Measure *up* from the end of the shoulder *cutting line* the 1/4" or 1/2". Mark on the worksheet. (Fig. 7-19)

Square shoulders

Fig. 7-18

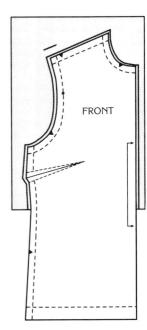

Outline pattern on worksheet.

Measure up 1/4" or 1/2" from end of shoulder cutting line.

FRONT

Fig. 7-19

3. Place a pin where the neckline and shoulder stitching lines cross. **Pivot** the pattern until the *cutting line* meets the increase mark. With the red pen, outline the new shoulder cutting line. (Fig. 7-20)

4. Keep the pattern pivoted. Transfer the pivot pin to where the shoulder and armhole stitching lines cross. **Pivot** the pattern so the *cutting line* meets the original outline at the underarm. (Fig. 7-21)

5. Trace the new armhole cutting line. Tape the pattern to the worksheet, matching the original outline to the old pattern cutting lines. Cut out the pattern, following the new cutting lines. (Fig. 7-22)

6. Repeat on the back pattern piece.

Pivot pattern
to meet original
outline at
underarm.

Outline new
armhole
cutting line.

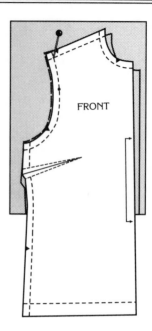

Fig. 7-21

Pivot pattern
to meet
increase mark.

Outline new
shoulder
cutting line.

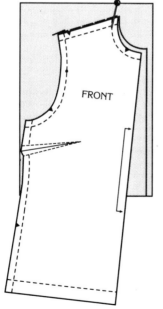

Fig. 7-20

Completed
alteration
on worksheet

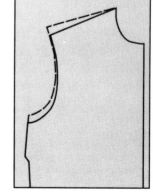

Fig. 7-22

Back Fitting Challenge #1: "How do I change the pattern to prevent tightness across the back?" (Fig. 7-23)

Tightness in the back of a ready-made or sewn garment is a common fitting complaint. Many of us buy a larger pattern size just to improve the fit in the back. But this results in a poor fit through the neck and shoulders. You can easily add additional room across the back without purchasing a larger pattern size.

Calculate the Change

The back of the pattern is automatically increased when the bustline is increased. One half of the amount added to the bustline is also added to the back width when you pivot. Fig. 7-24 shows how a 1" increase at the bustline also gives you a 1/2" increase across the back.

If you still need additional width across the back, or if you did not increase the bustline, measure the pattern to determine the change.

Check Your Measurement

Have someone assist you in taking an accurate Back Width Measurement. Use the same technique we used in Chapter 2 for the Front Width Measurement.

1. Measure across the back directly above the back arm crease from one side to the other side. (Fig. 7-25) Measure to the closest 1/4". To this measurement add 1-1/4" ease. (This is the standard ease in a blouse, dress, or top pattern. If making a jacket, add 1-1/2" ease.)

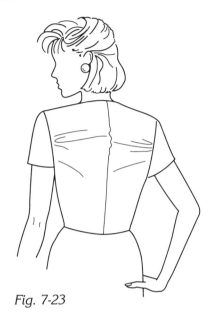

Fig. 7-23

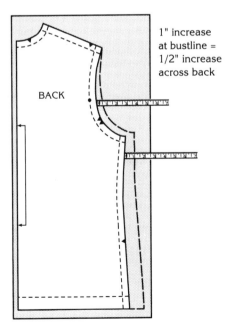

1" increase at bustline = 1/2" increase across back

BACK

Fig. 7-24

2. Hold the tape measure with the 1"
end to your left. Put your right thumbnail
on the measurement determined in Step
1. Fold the 1" end behind the tape measure to your thumbnail. Pinch the fold in
the tape measure with your left hand
and hold the 1" end securely against the
rest of the tape measure. This folding
gives you half your Back Width Measurement plus half the ease you need in
order to measure the back pattern half.
Still pinching the tape measure, turn it
upside-down, so the 1" end is to the
right.

3. Place the tape measure across the
pattern at the dot at the center of the
armhole, measuring from center back to
the armhole *stitching line*. (Remember,
if you increased the bustline, you should
be measuring your altered worksheet/pat-
tern.) The distance between the *1" end*
of the tape measure and the *armhole
stitching line* is the amount you need to
add across the back pattern half (1-1/8"
in Fig. 7-26). (When you cut out the pattern, adding on both sides of the back,
you automatically have the full ease you
need.)

Solution:

The same increase is added at the
center of the armhole and at the underarm. Extra room is needed in both areas
to give needed width for a broad back.

1. Place a worksheet under the *back*
pattern piece. With the black pen, outline the cutting lines on the worksheet.

2. Measure *out* the needed increase
from *both* the center of the armhole and
the underarm seam line. (Fig. 7-27)

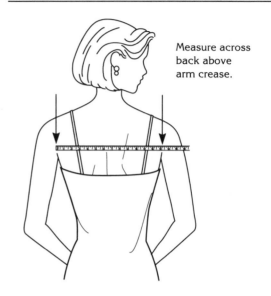

Measure across
back above
arm crease.

Fig. 7-25

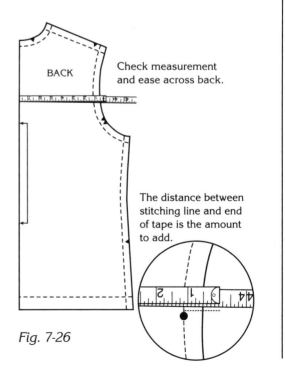

BACK

Check measurement
and ease across back.

The distance between
stitching line and end
of tape is the amount
to add.

Fig. 7-26

Outline pattern
on worksheet.

Measure out
increase from
center of
armhole and
underarm.

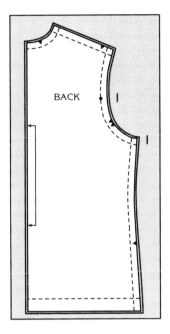

BACK

Fig. 7-27

Pivot pattern
to meet mark
at armhole
center.

Trace new
armhole to
center mark.

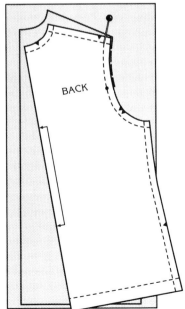

BACK

Fig. 7-28

3. Place a pin where the shoulder and armhole stitching lines cross. **Pivot** the pattern so the *cutting line* meets the first increase mark at the center of the armhole. With the red pen, trace the new armhole cutting line to the center mark on the worksheet. (Fig. 7-28)

4. Keep the pattern pivoted. Move the pivot pin to the dot on the stitching line at the center of the armhole. **Pivot** the pattern so the *cutting line* meets the in-crease mark at the underarm.

5. Outline the remaining armhole on the worksheet. Keep the pattern in this position. (Fig. 7-29)

6. Place the pin at the underarm where the stitching lines cross. **Pivot** the pattern to meet the original pattern

Pivot pattern
to meet mark
at underarm.

Outline remaining
armhole on
worksheet.

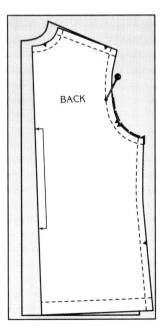

BACK

Fig. 7-29

waistline. Trace the new cutting line on the worksheet at the side seam. (Fig. 7-30)

7. Tape the pattern to the worksheet, matching the original outline to the old pattern cutting lines. Cut out the pattern, following the new cutting lines. (Fig. 7-31)

N *The new armhole cutting line is not as C-shaped, but it is the same length as the original pattern. Since the back side seam did not change in length, the front piece does not need any further alteration.*

Pivot pattern to meet original waistline.

Trace new side seam.

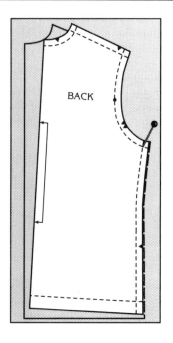

Fig. 7-30

Completed alteration on worksheet

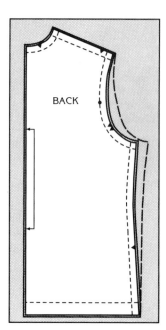

Fig. 7-31

CHAPTER 8
LENGTH SOLUTIONS

How do I:

- *lengthen the hemline on a one-piece dress pattern?*
- *shorten the hemline on a one-piece dress pattern?*
- *lengthen or shorten a skirt pattern?*
- *lengthen or shorten a fitted waist?*
- *lengthen the back of the pattern to fit a curved back?*
- *shorten the back of the pattern to fit a sway back?*
- *alter the skirt for a sway back?*

The traditional alterations used to lengthen a pattern involve slashing the pattern apart and spreading the pieces of the pattern to achieve the needed length. The opposite alteration, to shorten, is traditionally accomplished by taking a tuck in the pattern.

As stated in Chapter 1, these methods are workable, but many times the result is uneven side seams or uneven amounts added to or subtracted from the pattern. All the changes in this chapter will be made on a worksheet by **Sliding** the pattern up or down, following the grainline. It's a simple, yet accurate approach—the perfect solution for the busy woman.

Prepare to Fit

1. Cut out the front and back pattern pieces along the *cutting lines*. Press the pattern tissue pieces with a dry iron.

2. Cut two worksheets (lengths of wax paper, tissue paper, or a non-woven fabric like Pellon's® Tru-Grid®) as long as each pattern piece.

3. Organize your fitting tools:

- red and black permanent marking pens, fine-point
- pencil
- pins
- tape measure
- tape
- tracing wheel
- yardstick

Measure the Length

When working with a one-piece dress pattern, it is easiest to use the actual pattern pieces to check the length of the pattern.

1. Wear a full slip or leotard and tights.

2. Pin together the shoulder seams of the front and back pattern pieces, stacking the stitching lines. (Fig. 8-1)

N N *If the dress pattern has a stylized horizontal seam at the hipline or under the bustline, pin those pattern pieces together, too, stacking the stitching lines to achieve the total length of the pattern.*

3. Pin the pattern shoulder seam to the slip strap or leotard; the shoulder

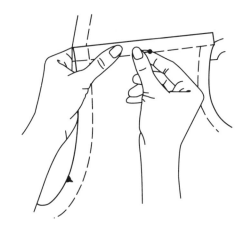

Pin pattern front to back, stacking stitching lines.

Fig. 8-1

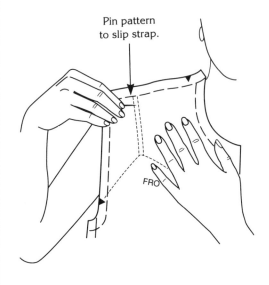

Pin pattern to slip strap.

FRO

Fig. 8-2

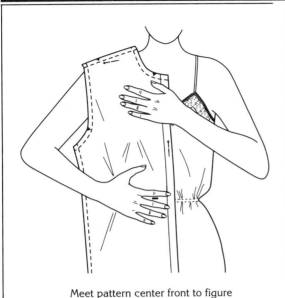

Meet pattern center front to figure center front. Pin to slip.

Fig. 8-3

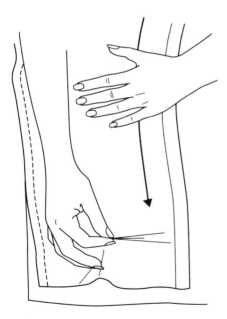

Pinch the pattern at desired length.

Fig. 8-4

line should be barely visible when looking in the mirror. (Fig. 8-2)

4. Meet the center front of the pattern to your center front. Pin to slip or leotard. Place a pencil mark at your waistline at the front and back. (Have someone help you mark the back.) (Fig. 8-3)

5. Walk the pattern down your figure. Pinch the pattern at the desired length. (Fig. 8-4)

6. Place a pencil mark on the pattern at the desired finished length.

7. Remove the pattern pieces from your figure and unpin the front and back pieces.

8. Your pattern may not have the hemline drawn but it gives the hem allowance (approximately 1-1/2"—2") at the bottom. Draw in the hemline parallel to the bottom cutting line.

9. Measure from the mark you made in Step 6 to the *hemline* you marked in Step 8. This is the amount you need to lengthen or shorten.

10. Make the same hemline marks on the back piece.

N **N** ***We lengthen or shorten patterns by sliding. This keeps the grainline undisturbed and evenly adds or subtracts length without distorting the cutting lines at the side seams.***

Hem Length Fitting Challenge #1:
"How do I lengthen the hemline on a one-piece dress pattern?"

Solution:

1. Place the front pattern piece on top of a worksheet. With the black permanent marker, outline *only* the bottom cutting line and 1" along the side seam and center front on the worksheet. (Fig. 8-5)

2. Extend the grainline on the pattern. Draw this extended grainline on the worksheet.

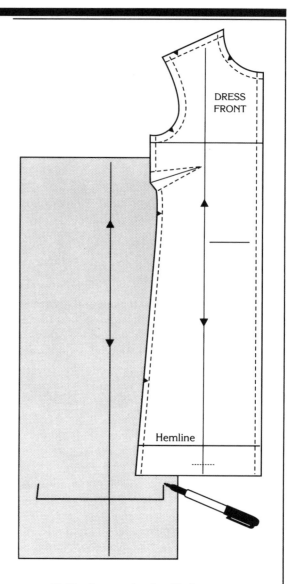

N *If you're using wax paper or tissue paper as a worksheet, use a tracing wheel and yardstick to trace over the grainline. The tracing wheel will perforate the wax paper or tissue paper, accurately marking the grainline.*

3. To lengthen the pattern, measure *up* on the worksheet from the *bottom cutting line* the needed amount and mark.

4. Place the pattern on the original bottom cutting line. **Slide** the pattern *up*, following the grainline, until the pattern meets the lengthening mark. (Fig. 8-6)

5. Outline the rest of the side seam and center front. (Fig. 8-7)

6. Without moving the pattern, tape it to the worksheet. Cut out the pattern, following the new cutting lines.

7. Apply the same steps to the back pattern piece.

DRESS FRONT

Hemline

Outline hem cutting line 1" along side seams and center front.

Extend grainline on pattern. Draw extended grainline on worksheet.

Fig. 8-5

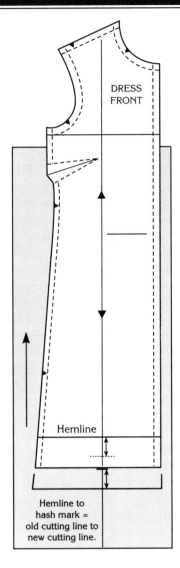

DRESS
FRONT

Hemline

Hemline to
hash mark =
old cutting line to
new cutting line.

Measure increase up from
hem cutting line and mark.

Slide pattern up to meet
lengthening mark.

Fig. 8-6

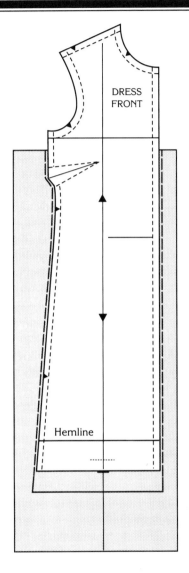

DRESS
FRONT

Hemline

Outline rest of pattern on
worksheet to finish alteration.

Fig. 8-7

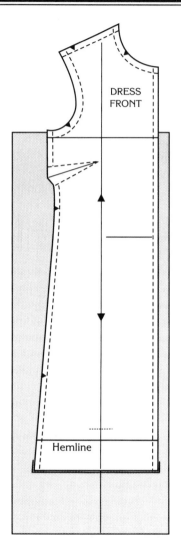

Outline hem cutting line and 1"
along side seams and center front.

Extend grainline on pattern. Draw
extended grainline on worksheet.

Fig. 8-8

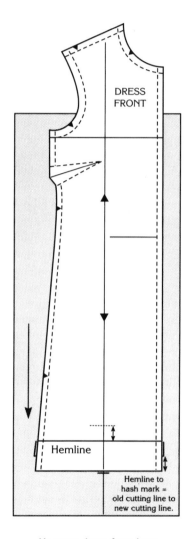

Hemline to
hash mark =
old cutting line to
new cutting line.

Measure down from hem
cutting line and mark.

Slide pattern down to
meet shortening mark.

Fig. 8-9

Hem Length Fitting Challenge #2: "How do I shorten the hemline on a one-piece dress pattern?"

Solution:

1. Place the front pattern piece on top of a worksheet. With the black permanent marker, outline *only* the bottom cutting line and 1" along the side seam and center front on the worksheet.

2. Extend the grainline on the pattern. Draw this extended grainline on the worksheet. (Fig. 8-8)

3. To shorten the pattern, measure *down* on the worksheet from the *bottom cutting line* and mark.

4. Place the pattern on the original cutting line. **Slide** the pattern *down* to meet the mark. (Fig. 8-9)

5. With the red pen, outline the rest of the pattern.

6. Tape the pattern to the worksheet. Fold up the longer pattern so the new cutting line is visible. Cut out the pattern, following the new outline. (Fig. 8-10)

7. Apply the same steps to the back pattern piece.

Hem Length Fitting Challenge #3: "How do I lengthen or shorten a skirt pattern?"

Solution:

To check the length, simply pin the pattern skirt front to your undergarments, matching and pinning center fronts and placing the waistline seam at your waistline. Walk the pattern down your figure as detailed in the preceding Measure the Length section.

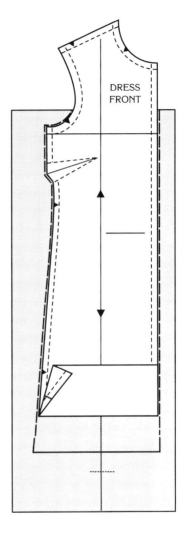

DRESS FRONT

Outline rest of pattern on worksheet to finish alteration.

Fig. 8-10

To alter the pattern, use the same steps as detailed for a one-piece dress in Length Fitting Challenges #1 and #2.

**Waist Length Fitting Challenge #1:
"How do I lengthen or shorten the
waist length on a dress with a fitted
waistline?"**

Solution:

If the waistline marks you made on
the tissue pattern (Fig. 8-3) indicate that
the front and back waistline length
needs to be *evenly* lengthened or shortened, alter the pattern using the **sliding**
technique.

Refer to Hem Length Fitting Challenge #1 and #2. Instead of making the
change at the hemline bottom cutting
line, make the alteration at the waistline
bottom cutting edge. Alter both front
and back pattern pieces by **sliding** the
pattern *up* to lengthen or *down* to
shorten the waistline length.

**Waist Length Fitting Challenge #2:
"How do I lengthen the back of the
pattern to fit a curved back?"**

The back waist length of the back pattern piece needs to be longer for figures
with a curve to the back or with rounded
shoulders. Check the pattern pieces. If
the back waistline length is marked
lower than the front (Fig. 8-3), or if the
fit of a ready-made has stress wrinkles
between the neck and waistline, the
back length needs to be longer.
(Fig. 8-11) You can determine the alteration amount in two ways.

Method A: Compare Your Waistline Marks

- Measure the difference between
  your front waistline (marked on the
  front pattern piece) and your back

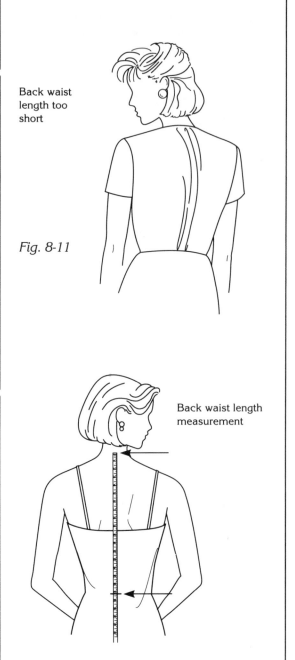

Back waist
length too
short

Fig. 8-11

Back waist length
measurement

Fig. 8-12

Increase mark

Outline pattern on worksheet.

Measure increase up from cutting line at center back.

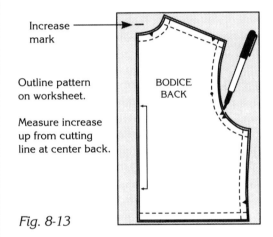

BODICE BACK

Fig. 8-13

Slide pattern up to meet increase mark.

Outline longer center back and new neckline.

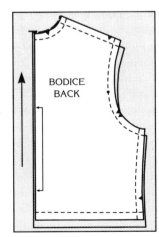

BODICE BACK

Fig. 8-14

waistline (again, marked on the back pattern piece). (Fig. 8-3)

- The difference between the two measurements is the amount to add to the back piece

Method B: Measure Your Back Length

- Measure from the bone at the base of the neck to the waistline. (Fig. 8-12)
- Compare your measurement to the measurement printed on the back of the pattern envelope. If the difference is 1/2" or more, alter the back piece.

N N *The next two alterations are made only on the back piece. The changes will be made at the neckline so that the side seams remain the same length as the front pattern side seams.*

Solution:

1. Place the *back* pattern piece on top of a worksheet. Outline the pattern cutting lines, using the black permanent marker.

2. Measure *up* from the *cutting line* at the center back the needed length. Place a mark on the worksheet. (Fig. 8-13)

3. **Slide** the pattern *up* to meet the increase mark.

4. With the red pen, outline the longer center back and also the neckline cutting lines. (Fig. 8-14)

5. Keep the pattern in the raised position. Place a pin where the neckline and shoulder stitching lines cross. **Pivot** the

Pivot pattern
to meet original
outline at end
of shoulder.

Outline new
shoulder cutting
line.

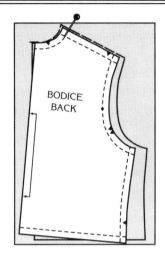

Fig. 8-15

Completed
alteration

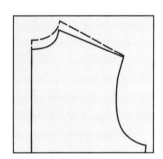

Fig. 8-16

Lenghten dart
legs if shoulder
seam has a dart.

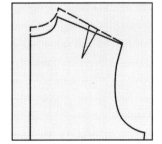

Fig. 8-17

pattern so the *cutting line* meets the original outline at the end of the shoulder.

6. Outline the new shoulder seam cutting line. (Fig. 8-15)

7. Tape the pattern to the worksheet, matching the original outline to the old pattern cutting lines. Cut out the pattern, following the new outline. (Fig. 8-16) If the pattern has a shoulder dart, as in a blazer, follow these same steps. After altering, simply extend the dart legs to meet the new shoulder cutting line. The shoulder dart will be made longer; this is needed for long, round shoulders. (Fig. 8-17)

Waist Length Fitting Challenge #3: "How do I shorten the back of the pattern to fit a sway back?"

The back pattern piece needs to be shorter for figures with very erect posture or a sway back. In either instance, wrinkles gather at the back waistline, indicating that the back waist length is too long. (Fig. 8-18)

Measure Your Back Length

- Measure from the bone at the base of the neck to the waistline.

- Compare your measurement to the measurement printed on the back of the pattern envelope. If the difference is 1/2" or more, alter the back piece. This alteration is commonly referred to as a *sway back* change.

Back waist
length too
long

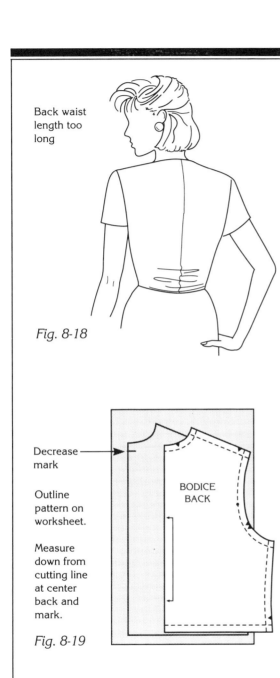

Fig. 8-18

Decrease
mark

Outline
pattern on
worksheet.

Measure
down from
cutting line
at center
back and
mark.

Fig. 8-19

Slide pattern
down to meet
decrease mark.

Outline new
cutting line
at neckline.

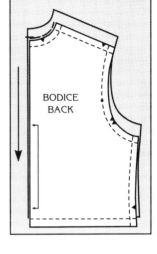

Fig. 8-20

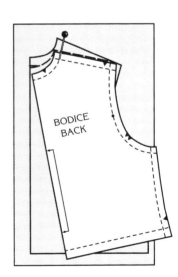

Fig. 8-21

Solution:

1. Place the *back* pattern piece on top of the worksheet. Outline the pattern cutting lines on the worksheet.

2. Measure *down* from the *cutting line* at the center back the needed decrease. Place a mark on the worksheet. (Fig. 8-19)

3. Slide the pattern *down* to meet the decrease mark. With the red pen, outline the new cutting line at the neckline. (Fig. 8-20)

4. Keep the pattern in the lowered position. Place a pin where the neckline and shoulder stitching lines cross. **Pivot** the pattern so the *cutting line* meets the original outline at the end of the shoulder seam.

Completed alteration on worksheet.

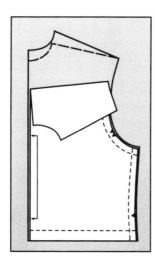

Fig. 8-22

5. Outline the new shoulder seam cutting line. (Fig. 8-21)

6. Tape the pattern to the worksheet, matching the original outline to the old pattern cutting lines. Fold back the pattern so the new outline is visible. Cut out the pattern, following the new cutting lines. (Fig. 8-22)

 In both cases, the pattern back was altered, either for a shorter or longer length, but the alteration did not change the shape of the neckline, allowing the collar to fit the pattern without any alterations. Also, the front and back pattern pieces will meet at the underarm seam, even though the back length was altered.

Waist Length Fitting Challenge #4: "How do I alter the skirt for a sway back?"

Horizontal fold wrinkles at the center back of the skirt are a common indicator of the *sway back.* (Fig. 8-23) The skirt back pattern can easily be changed to eliminate the wrinkle. A ready-made skirt can also be altered, using the same principles.

Refer to the Wrinkle Chart in Chapter 11, which explains whether wrinkles are folds or pulls.

Calculate the Change

It is impossible to measure the sway of the back. The easiest and most accurate way to determine the amount to

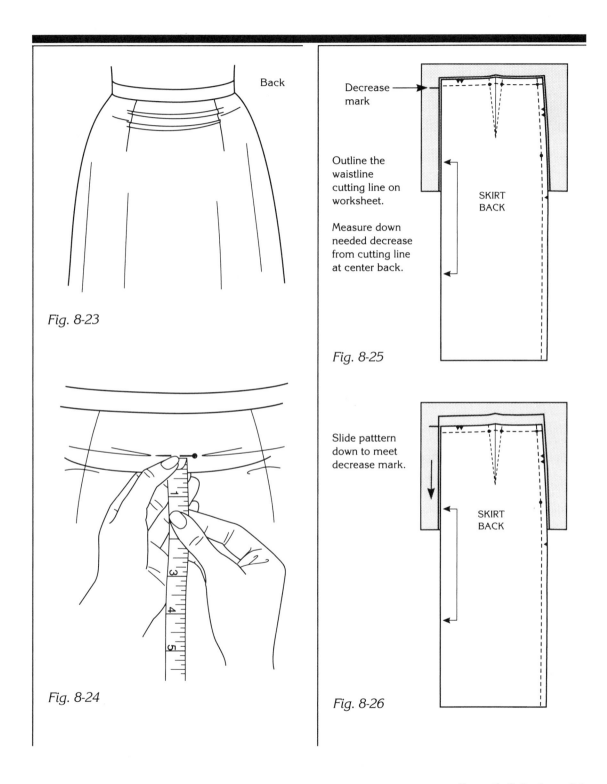

Back

Fig. 8-23

Fig. 8-24

Decrease mark

Outline the waistline cutting line on worksheet.

Measure down needed decrease from cutting line at center back.

SKIRT BACK

Fig. 8-25

Slide patttern down to meet decrease mark.

SKIRT BACK

Fig. 8-26

subtract at the center back is to check the fit on an existing skirt.

- If horizontal wrinkles appear below the waistline, pinch the extra fabric and pin out the fullness of the wrinkle at the center back.
- Measure the depth of the wrinkle. *Double* the amount to determine the excess length. (Fig. 8-24)

Solution:

1. With the black pen, outline the waistline, side seam, and center back cutting lines on the worksheet.

2. Measure *down* the needed decrease from the *cutting line* at the center back. (Fig. 8-25)

3. **Slide** the pattern *down* to meet the decrease mark. (Fig. 8-26)

4. Keep the pattern in the lowered position. Place a pin where the waistline and center back stitching lines cross. **Pivot** the pattern so the *cutting line* meets the original outline at the waistline side seam. (Fig. 8-27)

5. With the red pen, outline the new waistline cutting line.

6. Tape the pattern to the worksheet, matching the original outline to the old pattern cutting lines. Fold back the pattern so the new outline is visible. Cut out the pattern, following the new cutting line. (Fig. 8-28)

N
N *You can also make this change on zippered skirts you've sewn or bought. See Chapter 11, page 114.*

Fig. 8-27

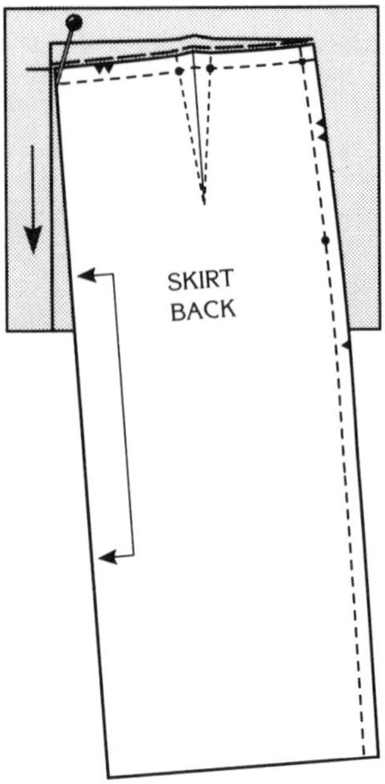

SKIRT BACK

Pivot pattern to meet original outline at waistline side seam.

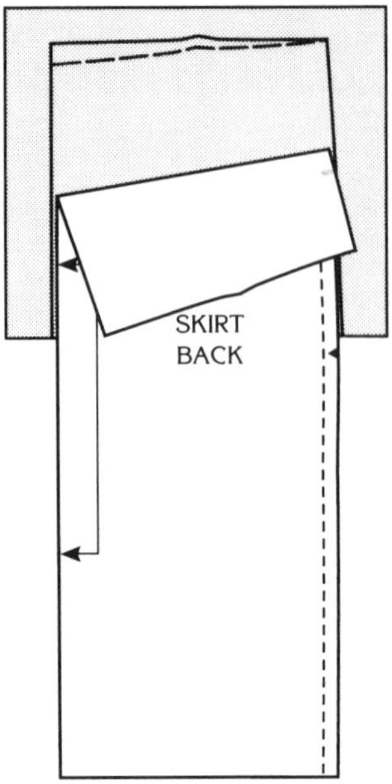

Completed alteration on worksheet.

SKIRT BACK

Fig. 8-28

CHAPTER 9
COMBINING ALTERATIONS

Tape worksheet of first alteration to pattern.

Trim worksheet following new cutting lines.

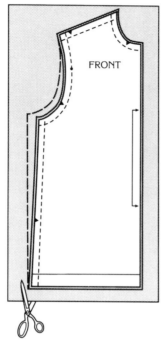

Fig. 9-1

Place second worksheet under pattern.

Outline pattern using new cutting lines.

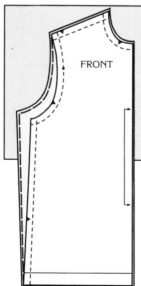

Fig. 9-2

So far, you have learned individual pattern alterations. Since many of us need two or more changes on our patterns, it is important to learn how to combine changes.

The Two-Step Approach

For beginners, the Two-Step Approach is the easiest way to combine alterations. You can make these changes in almost any order. As an example of this approach, I'll show you the changes of increasing the bustline and adjusting for square shoulders.

These are general. For detailed instruction, see the individual chapters.

1. Tape the worksheet of the first alteration to the pattern. This shows the alteration made to increase the bustline.

2. Trim the worksheet following the *new* cutting lines. (Fig. 9-1)

3. Make the second alteration by placing a second worksheet under the altered pattern. Outline the altered pattern using the *new* cutting lines from the first worksheet. (Fig. 9-2)

4. Alter as needed for the second alteration. In this example, a square shoulder alteration was made on the pattern.

5. When the second alteration is complete, tape the pattern to the worksheet on the old pattern cutting lines. Trim the worksheet, following the new cutting lines. (Fig. 9-3)

6. Make the same changes on the back pattern piece.

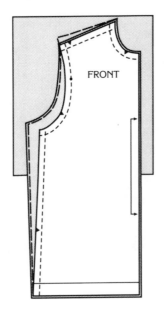

Make second alteration as needed.

Trim worksheet following new cutting lines.

FRONT

Fig. 9-3

The One-Step Approach

After becoming familiar with **Pivot and Slide Techniques**, you'll find that two or more alterations can be made on the same worksheet. This is a time-saving way to make pattern changes quickly, but you must follow a specific order.

One-Step Front/Back Alteration Order

For accuracy, when combining alterations in the One-Step Approach on front and back pieces, follow this order:

1. Hem
2. Center (front or back)
3. Neckline
4. Shoulder
5. Armhole/Back Width
6. Bustline
7. Waistline
8. Hipline

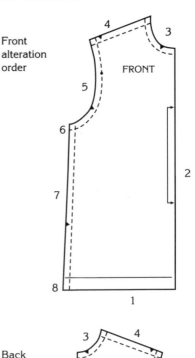

Front alteration order

FRONT

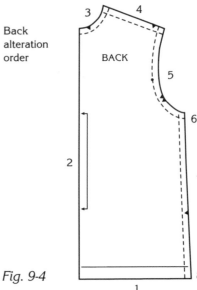

Back alteration order

BACK

Fig. 9-4

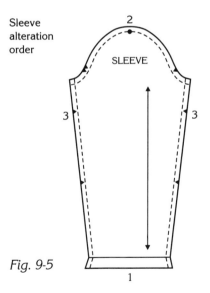

For the most part, on the front piece you'll be working counter-clockwise and on the back piece you'll be working clockwise.

Sleeve Alteration Order

When altering sleeves, the order is slightly different, since there is not a center front or back. Here's the sequence for the sleeve (Fig. 9-5):

1. Hem
2. Cap
3. Side seams

If you were changing the sleeve by altering the length and increasing the width, the length change would be made first at the hem, followed by the increased width change to the sleeve.

Sleeve alteration order

Fig. 9-5

Some Typical Alterations

Let's look at some typical alterations, so you can see what order you should use. These are general directions. For detailed instruction, consult the individual chapters.

One-Step Approach: Altering for Square Shoulders and Increasing the Bustline

1. Outline the front pattern on the worksheet.

2. Mark the worksheet for both alterations. (Fig. 9-6)

3. On the front piece work **counter-clockwise**, starting with the square shoulder alteration.

4. **Pivot** the pattern to meet the square shoulder mark above the end of

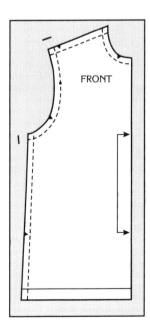

Outline pattern on worksheet.

Mark for both alterations.

Fig. 9-6

the shoulder seam. Outline the new cutting line of the shoulder. (Fig. 9-7)

5. Keeping the pattern pivoted, move the pivot pin to the shoulder pivot point.

6. **Pivot** the pattern to meet the bustline increase mark. Outline the new armhole cutting line. (Fig. 9-8)

7. Keeping the pattern pivoted, move the pivot pin to the underarm pivot point. **Pivot** the pattern so the *cutting line* meets the original waistline.

8. Outline the cutting line between the underarm and the waistline.

9. Tape the pattern to the worksheet on the old cutting lines. Cut out the pattern, following the new outline marks. (Fig. 9-9)

10. Repeat the steps on the back pattern piece, working clockwise.

Pivot pattern to meet bustline increase mark.

Outline new armhole cutting line.

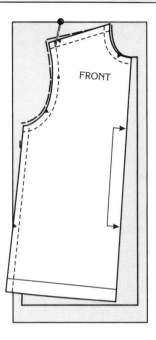

Fig. 9-8

Pivot pattern to meet square shoulder mark.

Outline new cutting line at shoulder.

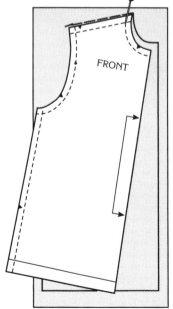

Fig. 9-7

Completed bustline and square shoulders alteration on worksheet.

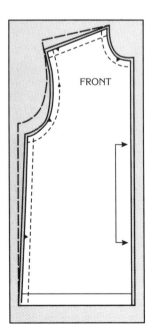

Fig. 9-9

One-Step Approach: Lengthening the Sleeve and Increasing the Sleeve Width

These are general directions. For detailed instruction, consult the individual chapters.

1. Outline *only* the hem area on the worksheet. Extend the grainline on the worksheet.

2. Measure *up* from the bottom the needed hemline increase. Mark on the worksheet.

3. **Slide** the pattern *up*, following the grainline to meet the increase mark.

4. Outline the rest of the pattern. (Fig. 9-10)

5. Measure out the needed increase on each side of the underarm.

6. Place a pin in the stitching line at the cap of the sleeve.

7. **Pivot** to meet the increase mark at one of the side seams. Trace one half of the cap and 1" around the corner.

8. Keeping the pattern pivoted, move the pivot pin to the underarm at the pivot point. **Pivot** the pattern to meet the side seam cutting line near the hemline.

9. Place the pattern in the original position from Step 4. Repeat Steps 6 to 8 on the other half of the sleeve.

10. Tape the worksheet to the pattern, matching the cap areas. Follow the new outlines and fold back the pattern piece at the hem area when cutting. (Fig. 9-11)

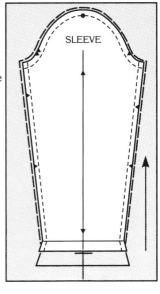

Outline hem and extend grainline on worksheet.

Measure increase up from hemline and mark. Slide pattern up to meet mark.

Outline pattern.

Fig. 9-10

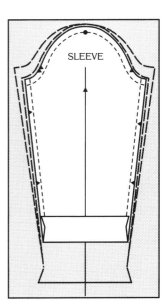

Completed alterations on worksheet.

Fig. 9-11

One-Step Approach: Lengthening the Back and Increasing the Bustline and Hipline

When you are experienced at Pivot and Slide Techniques and with the One-Step Approach, these are the only directions you'll need.

These are abbreviated directions. For detailed instruction, consult the individual chapters.

In this example, altering the back length would come first, followed by increasing the bustline and then increasing the hipline.

1. Start with the *back* piece. Outline the cutting lines on a worksheet and mark the needed changes for a longer back length, increased bustline, and increased hipline.

2. **Slide** the pattern *up* to lengthen the back. (Fig. 9-12)

3. **Pivot** the pattern twice to increase the bustline and hipline. (Fig. 9-13)

4. Tape the pattern to the worksheet. Cut out the pattern, following the new cutting lines. (Fig. 9-14)

The longer back length change is made only on the back piece. Alter the front piece only at the hipline and bustline. The side seams and armhole lengths remain the same on both front and back.

Whatever your fitting needs, the pattern alterations can be combined by either using the One-Step or Two-Step Approach. For beginners, the Two-Step Approach may be the easiest. After becoming proficient with the steps, combine the steps on the same worksheet to save time.

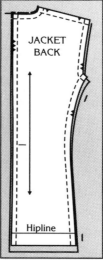

Slide pattern up to meet mark.

Outline neckline and longer center back.

Fig. 9-12

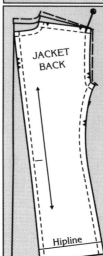

Pivot pattern to meet mark at underarm seam.

Outline new armhole.

Fig. 9-13

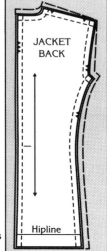

Fig. 9-14

Completed alterations on worksheet.

CHAPTER 10

FITTING SOLUTIONS ON STYLIZED PATTERNS

How do I:

- *alter princess-style patterns?*
- *alter a pattern with dolman or kimono sleeves, or a dropped shoulder?*
- *alter the bustline on a raglan pattern?*
- *alter the sleeve on a raglan pattern?*
- *alter the bustline on shoulder yokes?*
- *alter patterns with decorative features like tucks?*

Pivot and Slide Techniques make it easily possible for you to add many inches to your pattern and still maintain its design lines. Until now, you have been working on classic-style patterns. But you will also need to alter stylized patterns, such as shoulder yokes, dolman sleeves, or princess lines. These are equally easy to alter.

Please do not attempt these until you have practiced altering the bustline, waistline, hipline, sleeves, and length on classic-style patterns. These are general directions on pivoting and sliding. For specific directions, see the appropriate earlier chapters.

Fitting Challenge #1:
"How do I make alterations on princess-style patterns?"

A princess-style pattern has four main pattern pieces: center front, side front, center back, and side back. This styling with its numerous vertical seams is extremely flattering, especially on full-busted sizes. Most importantly, many inches can be added evenly to the multiple side seams without changing the style (and without using Extra Extensions).

Calculate the Change

Divide the needed increases at bustline, waistline, and/or hipline by the 12 cut edges. (There are six vertical seams. Each seam has two cut edges, resulting in 12 cut edges.)

For example, if 6" were needed at the bustline, 1/2" would be added at each side seam. Also, divide the waistline and/or hipline increases by 12. (*Note:* Your pattern may have a center back seam, but we do not alter at center back or center front. It throws the grain off.)

Solution:

1. Pin the pattern pieces together at the underarm, stacking the stitching lines. Also pin back to side back and front to side front.

2. Mark the underarm on the side front and side back pattern pieces. Extend this underarm mark to the center front and center back pieces as illustrated, keeping the line perpendicular to the grain line. Separate the four pattern pieces. (Fig. 10-2)

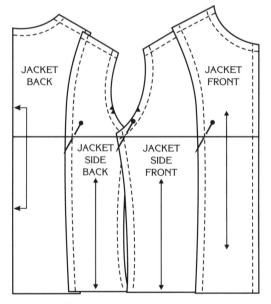

Increasing the hipline on princess styles usually gives enough room for your waist. Measure the altered worksheet at the waistline to check.

3. Place each of the pattern pieces on top of a worksheet. Outline the cutting lines using the black permanent marking pen.

4. Measure out the needed bustline increase from each side edge at the underarm line and hipline. (Fig. 10-3 and -4)

Pin pattern pieces together at underarm, stacking stitching lines.

Fig. 10-2

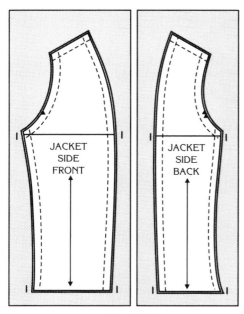

Fig. 10-3

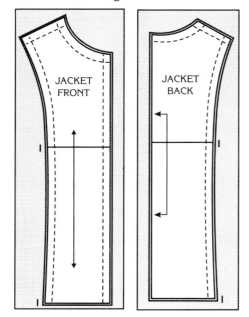

Measure needed bustline increase out from each side edge at underarm line and hipline.

Fig. 10-4

Side Front & Side Back Pattern Pieces

5. Alter the pattern at the *side seam* by placing a pivot pin where the shoulder and armhole stitching lines cross. **Pivot** the pattern to meet the increase mark at the underarm area. With the red pen, outline the new armhole cutting line. (Fig. 10-5)

6. Keeping the pattern pivoted, move the pivot pin to the underarm where the stitching lines cross. **Pivot** the pattern to meet the increase mark at the hipline. Outline the new cutting line at the side seam between the underarm and hipline. (Fig. 10-5)

7. Place the pattern back in the original position. To increase the *inner seam*, place the pivot pin where the shoulder and inner stitching lines cross. **Pivot** the pattern to meet the increase mark at the underarm line. Outline the new cutting line between the shoulder and underarm. (Fig. 10-6)

8. Keeping the pattern pivoted, move the pivot pin to the stitching line at the underarm. **Pivot** the pattern to meet the increase mark at the hipline. Outline the new cutting line at the side seam between the underarm and hipline. (Fig. 10-6)

9. Tape the pattern pieces to the worksheets, matching the old cutting lines. Cut out the pattern, following the new cutting lines. The completed changes are shown in Fig. 10-7.

Center Front and Center Back Pattern Pieces

10. To increase the *inner seam*, place a pin where the shoulder and inner

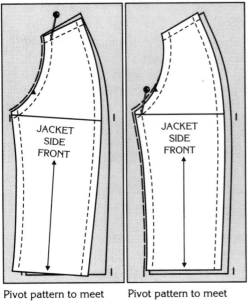

Pivot pattern to meet
mark at underarm.

Pivot pattern to meet
mark at hipline.

Fig. 10-5

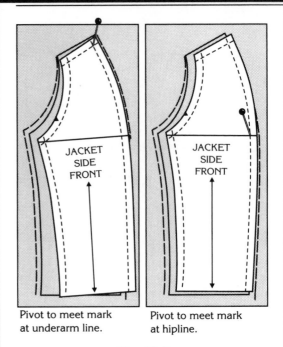

Pivot to meet mark
at underarm line.

Pivot to meet mark
at hipline.

Fig. 10-6

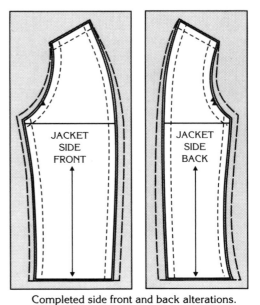

Completed side front and back alterations.

Fig. 10-7

seam stitching lines cross. **Pivot** the pattern to meet the increase mark across from the underarm line. With the red pen, outline the new cutting line between the shoulder and increase mark. (Fig. 10-8)

11. Keeping the pattern pivoted, move the pivot pin to the stitching line at the underarm mark. **Pivot** the pattern to meet the increase mark at the hipline. Outline the new cutting line at the side seam between the underarm and hipline. (Fig. 10-8)

12. Tape the pattern pieces to the worksheets, matching the old cutting lines. Cut out the pattern following the new cutting lines. (Fig. 10-9)

Another princess style has seams that lead into the armhole above the bustline. Called the military princess, it is altered the same way—by pinning the pattern pieces together at the underarm and drawing a line across all pattern pieces, as in Fig. 10-2, to determine where to mark the bustline increase marks.

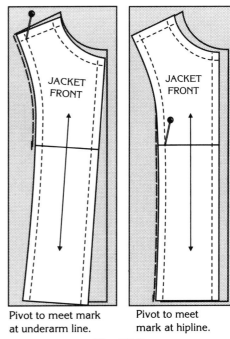

Pivot to meet mark at underarm line.   Pivot to meet mark at hipline.

Fig. 10-8

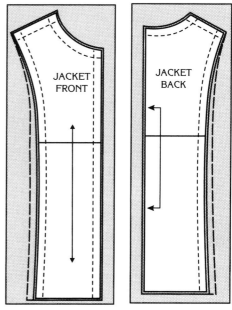

Fig. 10-9

Completed center front and back alterations.

Fitting Challenge #2:
"How do I alter the bustline on a pattern with dolman or kimono sleeves, or a dropped shoulder?"

Solution:

Dolman sleeves, kimono sleeves, and dropped shoulders can be altered using pivoting techniques. But with all of these styles, armhole placement is not evident; therefore, before altering, the armhole placement must be marked on this stylized pattern.

1. Place a classic blouse pattern of the same size with a basic armhole shape on top of the stylized pattern (dolman, kimono, or dropped shoulder). Match the waistlines and center fronts. Don't worry too much about matching the neckline and shoulder areas—this is a very forgiving style. Draw the armhole shape directly on the stylized pattern (Fig 10-10). (The stylized pattern will probably be larger than the basic blouse pattern.) Remove the basic blouse pattern.

2. Place the stylized pattern on top of the worksheet and with the black pen, outline the original pattern cutting line.

3. Measure *out* from the *cutting line* at the underarm area the needed increase. (If decreasing, measure *in* from the *cutting line*.) Place a mark on the worksheet.

4. Place a pin at the end of the shoulder where the line drawn in Step 1 and the shoulder stitching line intersect.

5. **Pivot** the pattern so the *cutting line* meets the increase mark at the underarm.

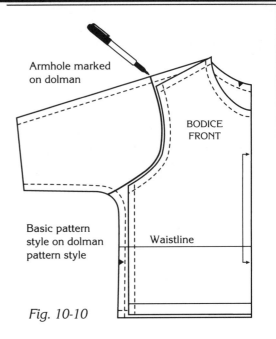

Armhole marked on dolman

BODICE FRONT

Basic pattern style on dolman pattern style

Waistline

Fig. 10-10

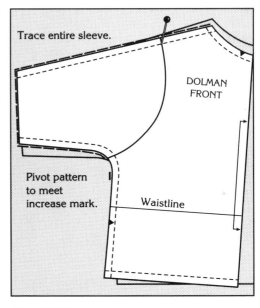

Trace entire sleeve.

DOLMAN FRONT

Pivot pattern to meet increase mark.

Waistline

Fig. 10-11

6. With the red pen, trace around the entire sleeve or dropped shoulder until you reach the increase mark. Keep the pattern in the pivoted position. (Fig. 10-11)

7. At the underarm, place the pivot pin on the stitching line of the stylized pattern. **Pivot** the pattern inward to meet the outline at the waistline. Trace the new underarm seam.

8. Tape the pattern to the worksheet, matching the original outline to the old pattern cutting lines. Cut out the pattern, following the new outline.

9. Apply the same steps to the back pattern piece.

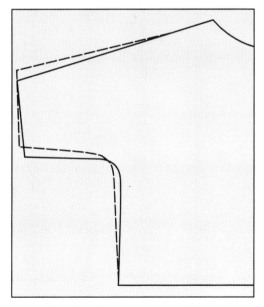

Completed alteration on worksheet

Fig. 10-12

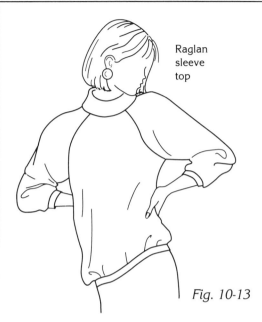

Raglan sleeve top

Fig. 10-13

Fitting Challenge #3:
"How do I alter the bustline on a raglan pattern?"

Solution:

1. Place the front pattern piece on top of a worksheet. With the black permanent marker, outline the pattern cutting lines on the worksheet.

2. Measure *out* from the *cutting line* at the underarm area the needed increase. (If decreasing, measure *in* from the *cutting line*.) Place a mark on the worksheet.

3. Place a pin at the neckline where the stitching lines cross.

4. **Pivot** the pattern so the *cutting line* meets the alteration mark. With the red pen, trace the new armhole cutting line. (Fig. 10-14)

5. Keep the pattern pivoted and place a pin at the underarm where the stitching lines cross. **Pivot** to meet the original outlined waist area. Trace the new cutting line between the underarm and waist. (Fig. 10-15)

6. Tape the pattern to the worksheet, matching the original outline to the old pattern cutting lines. Cut out the pattern, following the new outline. (Fig. 10-16)

7. Apply the same steps to the back pattern piece.

Pivot pattern to meet increase mark.

Trace new armhole.

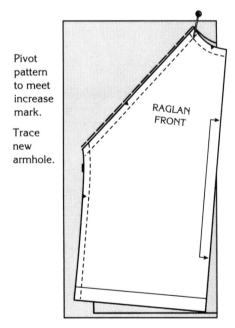

Fig. 10-14

Pivot pattern to meet outline at waist.

Trace side.

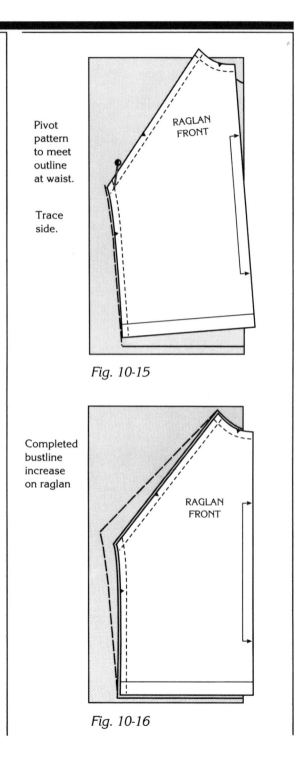

Fig. 10-15

Completed bustline increase on raglan

Fig. 10-16

Fitting Challenge #4:
"How do I increase a raglan sleeve?"

Solution:

Raglan sleeve alterations are similar to set-in sleeve changes. Instead of pivoting at the sleeve cap dot, the raglan sleeve is pivoted at the two neck edges.

1. Place the raglan sleeve on top of a worksheet. With the black permanent marker, outline the pattern cutting lines on the worksheet.

2. Measure *out* the needed increase from the side seam *cutting lines* at the underarm parallel to the side seams.

3. Place a pin where the neck edge and armhole stitching lines cross. **Pivot** the pattern so the *cutting line* meets the increase mark. With the red pen, outline the raglan armhole and 1" of the side seam. (Fig. 10-17)

4. Keep the pattern pivoted. Move the pivot pin to the stitching line where the raglan underarm and side seam cross. **Pivot** the pattern so the *cutting line* meets the original outline at the hem. Outline the new side seam cutting line.

5. Place the pattern in the original position. Repeat Steps 3 and 4 on the other side of the raglan sleeve.

6. Tape the pattern to the worksheet, matching the original outline to the old pattern cutting lines. Cut out the pattern, following the new outline. (Fig. 10-18)

Pivot pattern to meet increase mark. Outline raglan armhole.

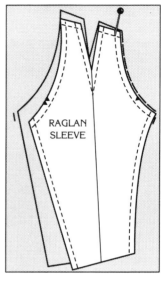

Fig. 10-17

Completed alteration on worksheet.

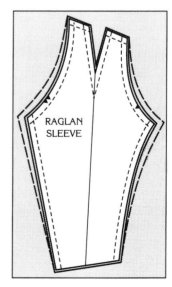

Fig. 10-18

Fitting Challenge #5:
"How do I alter the bustline on blouses with yokes across the shoulder?"

Solution:

1. Use a worksheet for each pattern piece, making sure the yoke worksheet is the same length and follows the same angles as the pattern. The yoke worksheet will be wider than the yoke.

2. Lap the yoke worksheet over the front worksheet 1-1/4", the amount of both seam allowances, and tape.

3. Pin the yoke pattern piece to the blouse front, stacking stitching lines.

4. Place the pattern pieces on top of the worksheets, matching the stacked seam allowances to the overlapped worksheets. With the black pen, outline the cutting line of the whole pattern on the worksheet. Measure *out* the needed increase from the *cutting line* at the underarm area. (If decreasing, measure *in* from the *cutting line*.)

5. **Pivot** the pattern from the armhole shoulder line, which is marked on the yoke pattern, so the *cutting line* meets the increase (or decrease) mark.

6. With the red pen, outline the armhole cutting line, starting at the shoulder line. Keep the pattern pivoted. Move the pivot pin to the underarm where the stitching lines cross and **pivot** back to the original waistline.

To alter the back, overlap the opposite end of the yoke worksheet to the back worksheet. Again, **pivot** at the armhole shoulder line and outline the new armhole beginning at the shoulder line.

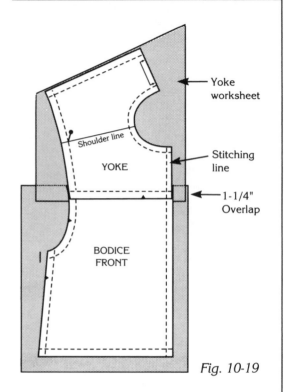

Fig. 10-19

Fitting Challenge #6:
"How do I alter when my pattern has decorative features, like tucks, pleats, or gathers?"

Solution:

Using the Busy Woman's Fitting Approach, you make alterations based on the *back of the pattern envelope* compared to your measurements. Thus, you do not need to worry about decorative details. You do not need to pin them in place on the pattern or worry about their measurement plus ease, as you must when you use other alteration methods. Just compare your measurements to the back of the pattern envelope and **pivot or slide** the pattern as necessary. KISS!

CHAPTER 11
FINE-TUNING THE FIT

Now that you've learned the **Pivot and Slide Techniques** that will help you make comfortable, flattering, well-fitting clothes, it's time to check your alterations on the garment itself.

We will baste your garment together, look for tell-tale wrinkles, analyze them, and recut both the garment and the altered pattern to eliminate the wrinkles. This is called fine-tuning the fit.

While this step may seem time-consuming, it's actually going to save you time in the future in three ways:

1. This is the only fit check you need for this garment. The wrinkles are easily eliminated, so once you transfer what you've learned from the garment to the pattern, you can complete the final sewing.

2. Once you make the recutting corrections on your classic-style pattern, you can use it freely, without checking the fit for each new garment.

3. Best of all, once you know what pattern changes your unique body requires, you will make them automatically on any pattern in the same size from the same company, *with no further measuring.*

 Without needing to measure and despite any style of pattern, I automatically make alterations for square shoulders, broad back, and larger hips. It's a terrific time-saver to know this key to fit.

Learn what changes you need to make on a classic-style blouse, jacket, skirt, and dress and after that, it's smooth sailing on *any* style.

 It's much easier to fine-tune the fit if a friend helps you. If you have to work alone, though, just do the best you can. Re-member, any improvement fits bet-ter than most ready-to-wear.

Check the Fit

Throughout this book, I've asked you to use a classic-style pattern for your first **Pivot and Slide** alteration project. Now this simple styling will make it eas-ier to check the fit.

Step 1: Machine-Baste

After cutting out the pattern, machine-baste these basic parts:

Blouse/Tops/Jackets (Fig. 11-1)

- darts
- shoulder seams (gather if necessary)
- center front or back and side seams
- sleeve underarm seam
- armhole seam for set-in sleeves

Dresses With Waistline Seams (Fig. 11-2)

- darts, pleats, or gathers
- shoulder seams (gather if necessary)
- center front or back and side seams of top and skirt
- sleeve underarm seam
- armhole seam for set-in sleeves
- waistline seam

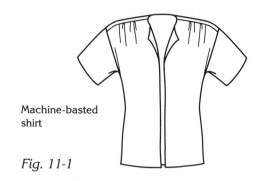

Machine-basted shirt

Fig. 11-1

Machine-basted dress

Fig. 11-2

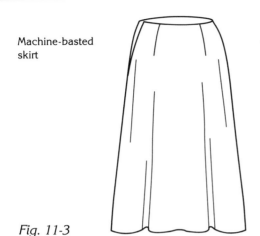

Machine-basted skirt

Fig. 11-3

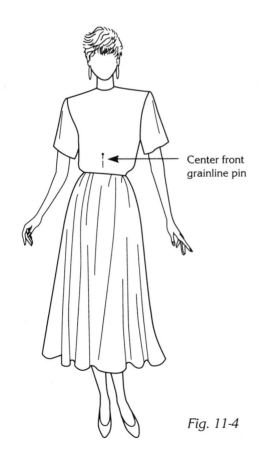

Center front grainline pin

Fig. 11-4

Skirt (Fig. 11-3)

- darts, pleats, or gathers
- side seams (do not close zipper opening)
- center front or back (do not close zipper opening)

Step 2: Try on the Garment

Blouses/Top/Jackets/Dresses

1. Pin in shoulder pads (if the pattern requires).

2. Try on the garment, pinning closed the center front or center back opening.

3. Match the center front of the garment to your center front. Pin to your undergarments. (Fig. 11-4)

Skirts

1. Sew 1" elastic together to fit your waistline. Put the elastic around your waistline.

2. Pin the skirt to the elastic, matching the 5/8" waistline stitching line to the center of the elastic. (Fig. 11-5)

3. Pin the zipper opening closed.

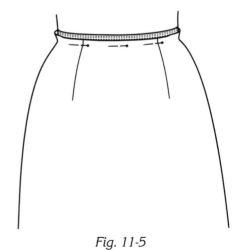

Fig. 11-5

Step 3: Check for Fold or Pull Wrinkles

Before analyzing the fit of your clothes, it is important to understand the different types of wrinkles. Most sewing books group wrinkles into three categories: horizontal, vertical, and bias. It is more useful to analyze first for folds or pulls and then look at their direction—horizontal, vertical, or bias. This means there are actually six wrinkles, not three:

Horizontal wrinkles that fold or pull

Vertical wrinkles that fold or pull

Bias wrinkles that fold or pull

A wrinkle that folds indicates too much fabric.

A wrinkle that pulls indicates too little fabric.

After identifying the wrinkles, change the garment and pattern pieces to correct them. To help you understand how these changes are made, an example from each of the wrinkle categories will be explained.

Since you purchased a pattern to fit your upper body according to the Front Width Measurement, checked the pattern for needed changes, and made any necessary alterations, very few, if any, of these wrinkles will occur. Congratulations!

	Fold Wrinkles: too much fabric	Pull Wrinkles: too little fabric
Horizontal	*Horizontal Fold Wrinkles* = *too much length*	*Horizontal Pull Wrinkles* = *not enough width*
Vertical	*Vertical Fold Wrinkles* = *too much width*	*Vertical Pull Wrinkles* = *not enough length*
Bias	*Bias Fold Wrinkles* (a combination of vertical & horizontal) = *too much length and width*	*Bias Pull Wrinkles* (a combination of vertical & horizontal) = *not enough length and* *not enough width*

Wrinkle Fitting Challenge #1:
"How do I eliminate horizontal fold wrinkles from my garment?"
(Fig. 11-7)

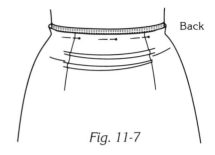

Fig. 11-7

Solution:

A common horizontal fold wrinkle occurs on skirts directly below the back waistline. This recutting step will be used as the example for all horizontal fold wrinkles.

Remember that a wrinkle with horizontal folds indicates too much length. You probably have a sway back.

Have someone help you fine-tune the fit on your garment. It's hard to fit the back yourself.

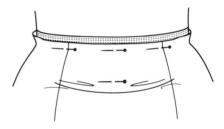

Fig. 11-8

1. Pinch the fold of extra fabric and place a pin at the base of it. This pins out the fold of the wrinkle. (Fig. 11-8)

2. Measure the depth of the wrinkle at the deepest part. Double the measurement. This is the amount of the wrinkle. (Fig. 11-9) Take off the garment. Undo the darts.

3. On the garment, measure down from the *cutting edge* at the center back the amount of the wrinkle (measured in Step 2). Place a pin in the fabric at this point (later referred to as the "marking pin").

4. Fold the skirt back in half, right sides together. Place the skirt back pattern on top of the actual skirt back. **Slide** the pattern down until the *cutting line* and *marking pin* meet. (Fig. 11-10a)

5. At the center back stitching line of the pattern, place a pin. **Pivot** the pattern so its waistline stitching line meets

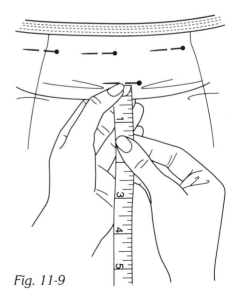

Fig. 11-9

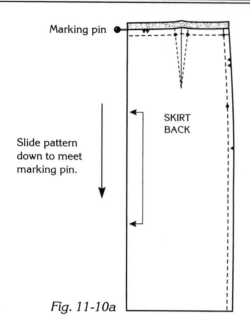

Marking pin

Slide pattern
down to meet
marking pin.

SKIRT
BACK

Fig. 11-10a

the actual waistline stitching line of the skirt at the side seams. (Fig. 11-10b)

6. Trim off the excess fabric, following the pattern cutting line. Save this fabric piece. (Fig. 11-10c)

7. Use the fabric piece to make the same recutting adjustment on the pattern piece. (Fig. 11-10d) For future sewing projects, alter the pattern for a sway back. See Chapter 8 for details.

It's not too late if you notice this wrinkle after the waistband has been attached. Release the back waistline stitches between the side seams and make the change detailed above. If the garment has a zipper, bartack on each side just below the new cut edge and trim off the excess zipper. You can also do this to ready-to-wear.

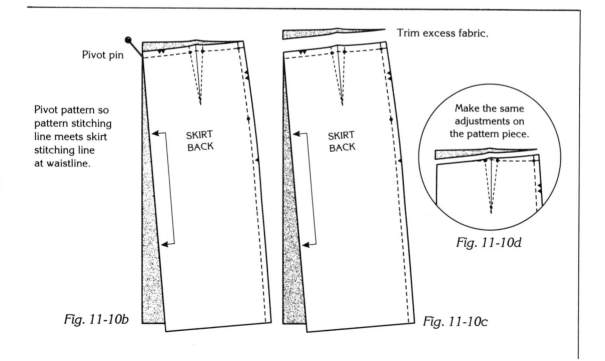

Pivot pin

Pivot pattern so
pattern stitching
line meets skirt
stitching line
at waistline.

SKIRT
BACK

Fig. 11-10b

Trim excess fabric.

SKIRT
BACK

Fig. 11-10c

Make the same
adjustments on
the pattern piece.

Fig. 11-10d

Wrinkle Fitting Challenge #2:
"How do I eliminate vertical fold
wrinkles from my garment?"
(Fig. 11-11)

Solution:

A common vertical fold wrinkle occurs across the back shoulder. This area of the pattern will be used as the example of recutting for any vertical fold wrinkles.

It's hard to fit the back yourself. Have someone help you. 1. Pinch out the fold of extra fabric to each side of the back, placing a pin at the base of the wrinkle. (Fig. 11-12)

2. Measure the depth of the wrinkle at the deepest part. Double this measurement. This is the amount that will be removed from each side of the armhole area.

3. Release the shoulder, armhole, and side seam stitches and remove the sleeves.

4. Meet the back fabric pieces right sides together.

5. On the garment at the center of the armhole, measure in from the *cut edge* the amount of the depth of the wrinkle (Step 2). Place a marking pin in the fabric. Also measure the same distance from the *cut edge* at the underarm. Again, place a marking pin in the fabric. (Fig. 11-13)

6. Place the back pattern on top of the fabric.

7. At the stitching line where the armhole and shoulder lines meet, place a pin. **Pivot** the pattern so the armhole *cutting line* meets the marking pin at the center of the armhole. Remove the

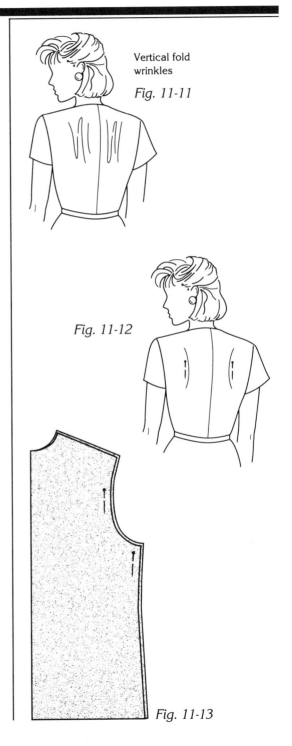

Vertical fold
wrinkles

Fig. 11-11

Fig. 11-12

Fig. 11-13

marking pin. Outline the new cutting line on the fabric between the shoulder and center of the armhole. (Fig. 11-14)

8. Keeping the pattern pivoted, move the pin to the stitching line at the center of the armhole. **Pivot** the pattern so the *cutting line* at the underarm meets the marking pin at the underarm. Outline the remainder of the armhole cutting line on the fabric between the center of the armhole and the underarm. (Fig. 11-15) Remove the marking pin.

9. At the underarm stitching line place a pin. **Pivot** the pattern so the *cutting line* meets the actual cut edge of the fabric at the waist area. Outline the new cutting line on the fabric from the underarm to the waistline.

10. Cut off the excess fabric, following the marking on the fabric. (Fig. 11-16)

11. Make the same recutting adjustments on the pattern piece. For future sewing projects, alter the pattern before cutting out.

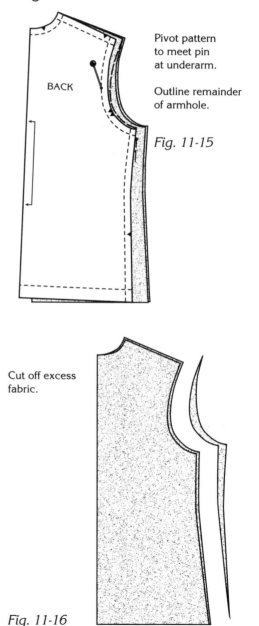

Pivot pattern to meet pin at underarm.

Outline remainder of armhole.

BACK

Fig. 11-15

Cut off excess fabric.

Fig. 11-16

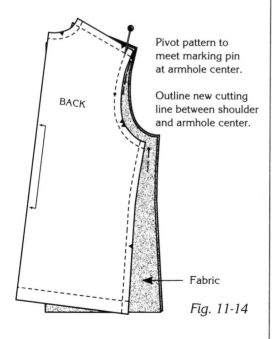

Pivot pattern to meet marking pin at armhole center.

Outline new cutting line between shoulder and armhole center.

BACK

Fabric

Fig. 11-14

Wrinkle Fitting Challenge #3: "How do I eliminate bias fold wrinkles from my garment?" (Fig. 11-18)

Solution:

A common bias fold wrinkle occurs at the armhole/underarm area. This area of the pattern will be used as an example of how to recut for all bias fold wrinkles.

Remember that bias fold wrinkles indicate too much length *and* width. In this example, the shoulder seam is too wide and the underarm seam is too long. It's hard to pin out wrinkles in this area by yourself. Have someone help you.

1. Since a bias fold wrinkle indicates too much length and width, it will be necessary to place two pins in the fabric: one pin pinning out the excess width and the second pin pinning out the excess length. In this example, the bias wrinkle is indicating that the shoulder seam is too wide and the underarm seam is too long. Place a pin at each area, pinning out the excess fabric. (Fig. 11-19)

2. Take off the garment. Measure the depth of the vertical fold wrinkle. Double the measurement. Measure the depth of the horizontal wrinkle. Again, double the measurement.

3. Release the armhole, shoulder, and underarm seams. Remove the sleeves. Fold the fabric front in half, right sides together.

4. To eliminate the excess shoulder width, measure in from the shoulder/armhole stitching line the amount of the vertical wrinkle (measured in Step 2). Place a pin vertically in the fabric at this point.

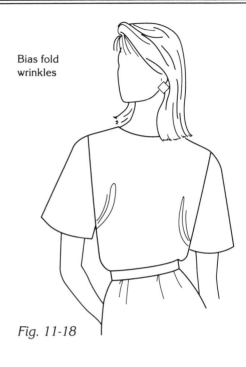

Bias fold wrinkles

Fig. 11-18

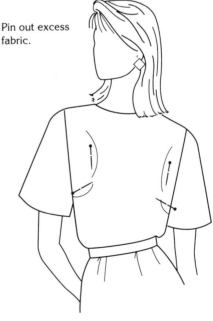

Pin out excess fabric.

Fig. 11-19

5. To eliminate the excess underarm length, measure down from the cutting line at the end of the shoulder the amount of the horizontal wrinkle. Place a pin horizontally in the fabric at this point. (Two pins are marking the changes.) (Fig. 11-20)

6. Place the front pattern on top of the fabric.

7. **Slide** the pattern along the shoulder seam until the *cutting line* at the end of the shoulder meets the vertical marking pin. (Fig. 11-21)

8. At the stitching line where the neckline and shoulder seams cross, **pivot** the pattern so the *cutting line* meets the horizontal marking pin at the end of the shoulder. Outline the new shoulder cutting line with a fabric marking pen. (Fig. 11-22)

9. Keep the pattern pivoted. At the stitching line where the shoulder and armhole seams cross, **pivot** the pattern so the *cutting line* meets the actual cut fabric at the underarm. Outline the new armhole cutting line with a fabric marking pen. (Fig. 11-23)

10. Cut off the excess fabric on both sides of the garment front. (Fig. 11-24)

11. Mark the same recutting adjustments on the pattern piece. Repeat on the back piece.

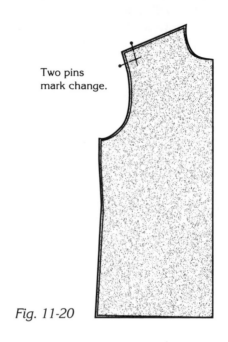

Two pins mark change.

Fig. 11-20

N N *If you're shortening more than 5/8", your pivot pin will be off the fabric. Merely move the pivot pin in on the stitching line.*

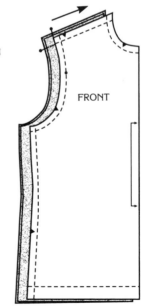

Slide pattern along shoulder seam to meet vertical marking pin.

FRONT

Fig. 11-21

Pivot pattern to meet horizontal marking pin. Outline new shoulder cutting line.

FRONT

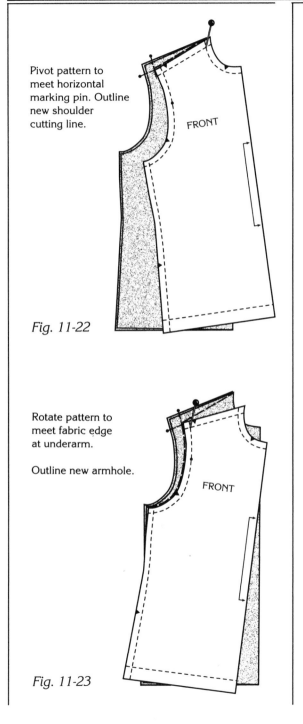

Fig. 11-22

Rotate pattern to meet fabric edge at underarm.

Outline new armhole.

FRONT

Fig. 11-23

N N These two recutting examples are the same steps used to alter the pattern for sloping shoulders and narrow shoulders. If it is necessary to recut your pattern for these wrinkles, please make these two alterations on your next project to avoid this recutting step. See Chapter 7.

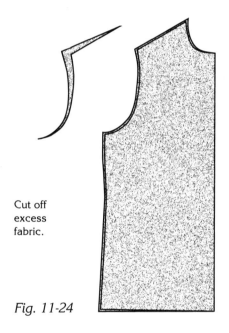

Cut off excess fabric.

Fig. 11-24

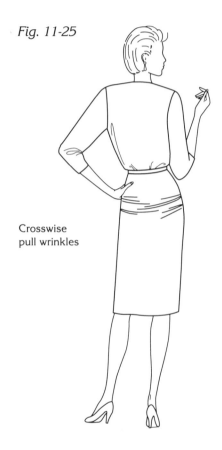

Fig. 11-25

Crosswise
pull wrinkles

Wrinkle Fitting Challenge #4: "How do I eliminate crosswise pull wrinkles from my garment?" (Fig. 11-25)

Solution:

Crosswise wrinkles that pull indicate that the garment is too tight in the width. You'll commonly find these wrinkles at the waistline, bustline, and/or hipline. Refitting crosswise pull wrinkles at the hipline will be demonstrated. Use the same procedure for all crosswise pull wrinkles.

1. Release the machine-basting at the side seams, below the waistline all the way to the hemline.

2. Restitch the seam by machine-basting a 1/4"—3/8" seam allowance. (This will give you 1" to 1-1/2" of additional room.)

3. Try on the skirt or dress to see if the wrinkles have been eliminated. If they are still evident and you have enough seam allowance, release the seam allowances, sewing a shallower seam. Use 15 stitches/inch. Zigzag the raw edges together and press the seam allowance to one side.

4. Mark the new stitching line on the pattern. For future sewing projects, increase the hipline. See Chapter 5.

Lengthwise pull wrinkles

Fig. 11-27

N N *When adding additional room to the hipline, make certain that the same increase is added all the way to the hemline. If a narrower seam allowance is taken just at the hipline area, the grainline will be distorted, resulting in the skirt bowing at the bottom and emphasizing the hips. (Fig. 11-26)*

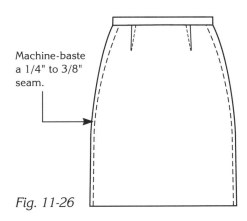

Machine-baste a 1/4" to 3/8" seam.

Fig. 11-26

Wrinkle Fitting Challenge #5: "How do I eliminate lengthwise pull wrinkles from my garment and pattern?" (Fig. 11-27)

Solution:

Common lengthwise pull wrinkles occur along the center back, indicating that the back length is too short. This fitting challenge will be used as an example for all lengthwise pull wrinkles.

1. Release the waistline stitches.

2. Sew a narrower seam allowance at the waistline, tapering to a normal seam allowance at the side seams. Mark the needed change on the pattern piece. (Fig. 11-28)

3. For future sewing projects, alter the pattern for a longer back length. See Chapter 8.

Mark narrower seamline on pattern piece.

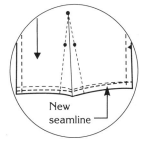

New seamline

Fig. 11-28

Wrinkle Fitting Challenge #6:
"How do I eliminate bias pull wrinkles from my garment and pattern?"
(Fig. 11-29)

Solution:

A common bias pull wrinkle occurs below the waistline, indicating that one hip is higher than the other. This wrinkle will be used as the example for recutting to fit all bias pull wrinkles.

Remember, bias pull wrinkles indicate that there is too little width and too little length.

1. Have someone help you. Unpin the skirt from the elastic around your waistline and release some of the side seam stitches to eliminate the wrinkles.

2. Sew a narrower side seam and mark a narrower waistline seam on the front and back of the higher hip side.

3. Make the same adjustments on the front and back pattern pieces. (Fig. 11-30)

4. For future sewing project, alter the pattern for a higher hip. See Chapter 5. (See also Robbie's note on page 47.)

N *After this first fitting for fine-tuning, you'll be able to make these changes on your next pattern before cutting out the pieces.*

Bias pull wrinkles

Fig. 11-29

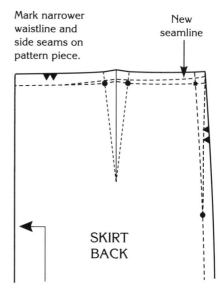

Mark narrower waistline and side seams on pattern piece.

New seamline

SKIRT BACK

Fig. 11-30

Index